Picture Perfect

1000 Journals, Arkitip, Bark, Jonathan Barnbrook, Ian Bilbey, Paul Bowman, Anthony Burrill, Carter Wong Tomlin, François Chalet, Cosmic Debris, eBoy, Designershock, Marion Deuchars, Simon Emery, Shepard Fairey, Lizzie Finn, Frost Design, Future Farmers, Gobler Toys, Jasper Goodall, Peter Grundy, Rian Hughes, Nathan Jurevicius, Kabeljau, Neasden Control Centre, Mark Pawson, Pixelhugger, Quickhoney, Rinzen, Andy Simionato, Ward Schumaker, THS, Garth Walker, Paul Wearing, Alex Williamson, Yee-Haw Letterpress Industries, Lawrence Zeegen

A RotoVision Book
Published & Distributed
by RotoVision SA
Route Suisse 9
CH-I295 Mies
Switzerland

RotoVision SA
Sales, Editorial & Production Office
Sheridan House
II2-II6a Western Road
Hove, East Sussex BN3 IDD, UK
Tel: +44 (0)I273 72 72 68
Fax: +44 (0)I273 72 72 69
ISDN: +44 (0)I273 73 40 46
Email: sales@rotovision.com
Web: www.rotovision.com

I0 9 8 7 6 5 4 3 2 I

ISBN 2-88046-754-3

Design by Visual Research: Ian Noble & Russell Bestley

Reprographics in Singapore by ProVision Pte. Ltd.
Printed in China by Midas Printing International Ltd.

Although every effort has been made to contact owners of
copyright material reproduced in this book, we have not
always been successful. In the event of a copyright query,
please contact the publisher.

Picture Perfect

Fusions of illustration & design

RotoVision

Contents

Introduction

Ian Noble

Ladies and gentlemen—Elvis has left the building

In graphic design circles it has become rather outmoded to discuss the impact of technology on the profession—despite its profound effects. Over the last decade designers have become fatigued by the ubiquitous ~~debate~~(s) and are now somewhat blasé about the dramatic transformation brought about in the media employed and in the range of opportunities now available.

Illustration—itself a part of graphic design, and certainly a discipline that is intrinsically linked to design through the process of commission and collaboration—has undergone a period of significant redefinition. The activity and practice of illustration and image-making has now grown to accommodate a wider range of approaches. While many illustrators continue to explore the more traditional media and materials within their practice, the discipline is now based on the opportunities presented by new technology. These new methods of working build upon the role of illustrator as both commercial artist and author.

A pretty picture

It would be wrong to single out the technological aspect of the discussion of illustration as the only factor at work within this process of transformation. There are others at work too. There existed a very 'pretty picture' for illustrators in the late 1970s and early 1980s. During that period, and its attendant boom and bust, illustrators prospered in tandem with their partners in design. The resultant effect of this was to create an unreasonable level of career expectation. It is certainly true that during this period a large number of influential illustrators emerged—many of whom are still active and vital today, such as Russell Mills, Sue Coe, and Ian Wright. But we should also remind ourselves of the many illustrators who took advantage of the 'good

times' to produce derivative and comfortable work which challenged little and created a climate that did not advance either the potential or craft of earlier work.

This situation, which persists in small part, has been exacerbated to some extent by the rigid and closed-down definitions of the activity from within the profession itself. In many cases this has denied the more eclectic and propositional approaches that today have become a significant part of contemporary image-making. As individuals have begun to produce work which extends the traditional activities of illustration—working in areas such as interactive media and television title sequences, for instance—they appear to have been regarded from within as stepping outside of their discipline.

>Shepard Fairey
Andre the Giant/Obey
the Giant sticker
(p.128/129, 130/131)

In recognizing the inter-relationship between design and illustration it is possible to chart the downturn in illustration's fortunes during the latter part of the last century as the practice of graphic design entered a period of significant change. As designers gained further access to technologies which allowed them to do more than ever before, the distinct boundaries between the various sub-sections of the profession of graphic design became blurred, allowing many to shift their approach at will.

What's my name?

Many within the profession have started to question how useful the terms 'illustrator' or 'illustration' are in describing the range of approaches and individuals currently involved in the creation of commercial images. This desire to move on and find a more useful title does at least indicate how aware those involved in the discipline are to the need for change. This book takes these factors as its starting point and aims to encapsulate the contemporary scene while acknowledging that illustration is in a constant state of transformation. As long ago as 1988, illustrator and educator Dan Fern called for a reassessment of the practice claiming: "We need to stand back and rethink illustration".

Contemporary culture and communication are largely image-based, and illustrators are better placed than most to take advantage of this situation. This does not necessarily mean a re-skilling or a loss of craft, but merely reinforces the need for a meaningful reappraisal of what illustration is. Rather than relying on old definitions—based upon the craft and media employed—the profession has begun to challenge the traditional hierarchies of commissioner, art director, and editor, with the illustrator working to their predetermined brief. An example of this is

provided by Rob Mason, Head of Illustration at Norwich School of Art, England, and himself a former student of Dan Fern. He observes that technology has allowed illustrators the potential to "take on typographic challenges" as easily as designers create imagery. This points to the changing nature of the activity—in particular the illustrator operating with a greater and more holistic role within projects, rather than a singular function concerned solely with producing the images.

The work featured on the following pages demonstrates how illustration has repositioned itself. As design writer, commentator, and former editor of Eye magazine Rick Poynor wrote, it is "illustration that challenges the limitations of the craft and through the intensity of its vision becomes as interesting as, or more interesting than, the purpose that inspired it". This approach is exemplified by illustrators such as Rian Hughes (p.62/63, 154/155), and Alex Williamson (p.34/35, 86/87), who are equally comfortable working across a broad range of media. Both create work such as typefaces and television title sequences, as well as the more familiar editorial illustrations found in magazines, books, and on record sleeves.

>Quickhoney
Saddam Hussein for The
Telegraph newspaper
(UK) 2003 (p.71, 117)

Others have used the potential of technology to find not only new ways to create images, but also to challenge our perceptions of illustration. Collectives such as THS in Germany (p.52/53) and Neasden Control Centre in the UK (p.27, 30/31, 64/65), and individuals such as Shepard Fairey in the US (p.09, 128/129, 130/131), have begun to redefine the forms that illustration can take and the manner in which illustrators work. Projects such as Beast magazine are based on the notion of collaboration, in both a local and remote fashion. The journal, which exists only in electronic form, offers new opportunities for illustrators to collaborate and exchange ideas—providing a platform from which to operate with a wider scope than existed previously.

Beast magazine, and THS, its creators, have provided a vehicle for illustrators to view their role as commentator on contemporary events and popular culture, and significantly the work is disseminated without the need for a commercial client. Shepard Fairey's Obey campaign has grown through 'unofficial' channels of communication, spreading around the world like a viral network; the message and concept continually replicated and interpreted by others.

Are you talking to me?

Illustrators are now getting commissions that until recently were given to graphic designers. The selection of work shown in this book shows that illustrators are now invading those areas which were traditionally the preserve of the graphic designer and typographer. The prolific body of work produced by Rian Hughes (p.62/63, 154/155), for example, includes many fonts that the design community have become used to seeing on the pages of design journals such as the US-based Émigré Magazine. An emerging aspect of this rethinking of the discipline has been the revisiting of earlier ideas of authorship so important in the traditional activities of illustration. For the practicing illustrator this authorial role comes from a need to explore ideas that could not exist within the constraints of commercial projects. This work often forms the basis of the illustrator's portfolio—the more experimental work situated alongside the 'real' projects and serving as a platform for new and different commissions.

This responsibility for content in self-initiated projects has allowed illustrators to embrace the many possibilities presented by new media more easily than graphic designers did during the last decade. For most, the notion of creating content, rather than working with given information, has been a struggle. A significant proportion of graphic design in recent years has been more concerned with the means of production than the content it expresses.

Illustrators and image-makers have used new technology to not only explore how it affects the construction of images, but also to extend the possibilities of the distribution of personal projects where the message or product does not necessarily originate from a commercial brief or client. There is also a negative aspect to this activity: in some cases it represents little more than a retreat from the commercial world, and the inadequacies of the art director whose indolence as a commissioner can result in stereotyping.

>Jonathan Barnbrook
Nixon font from the
Virus catalogue
(p.58/59, 90/91, 96/97)

This is the Typeface to tell lies in

The Two faces of

The Two faces of

This is the Typeface to tell the other countries whose culture you do not understand with. This is the Typeface to take over the United Nations with. This is the typeface to ignore human rights abuses in China with. This is the Typeface to not have a proper health system with. This is the Typeface which allows the gun lobby too much control resulting in thousands of innocent deaths a year with. This is the Typeface to talk about the lie of the American dream with.

Nixon

Nixon

Obey

This established tradition of self-generated project work has been updated and extended by projects such as Shepard Fairey's Andre the Giant (p.130/131). This campaign, which began in the US in 1989, explores both collaborative approaches and the viral nature of messages and visual communication. The Andre character, pictured on the posters, stencils, and stickers, is (sub) titled only with the words 'Obey' or 'Obey Giant'. Fairey describes this as "an experiment in phenomenology... a process of letting things manifest themselves". The message is left open to interpretation and meaning is often derived by its context and surroundings. This self-initiated project has grown and spread via a community of anonymous co-workers and collaborators who have replicated and interpreted the work around the world. Often it is flyposted or stickered in public spaces without permission. This subversion of the 'official' messages of advertisers is described by Fairey as an attempt to "simultaneously bring the viewer to question propaganda absorption and to encourage a democratization of the use of public space in a spectator democracy".

Someguy

The ongoing 1000 Journals project (p.36/37, 38/39) instigated and managed by Someguy, develops the idea of collaboration further. The project involves the placing of 1000 blank journals into the world. These are passed from person to person, each participant completing a number of pages before passing it on. The location of each journal can be tracked using the 1000 Journals website. When a journal is full it is returned to its point of origin and will be exhibited with the rest once the project is complete. While it has its roots in mail art networks of the recent past, the germ of the idea can be traced back to the 'Exquisite Corpse'—a technique employed by the surrealists based on old parlor games. The website describes the background further: "The goal is to provide methods for people to interact and share their creativity. If you ask a kindergarten class how many of them are artists, they'll all raise their hands. Ask the same question of 6th graders, and maybe one-third will respond. Ask high school grads, and few will admit to it. What happens to us growing up? We begin to fear criticism, and tend to keep our creativity to ourselves. Many people keep journals, of writing or sketching, but not many share them with people".

The role of technology within the 1000 Journals project and in many others featured in this book is significant: projects such as Beast magazine—the collaborative visual journal, now defunct, produced by THS (p.52/53)—and This is a Magazine, in Italy (p.78/79, 80/81), suggest new methods of disseminating work via the internet using PDF technology. While this work does not necessarily have a client, it allows all those involved, instigators, collaborators, and audience alike, to create a mutually beneficial network. This means illustrators can escape the ghetto of the personal portfolio, and that work gets seen.

>Rinzen
Differentville: Design
& Advertising Award
promotional materials
(p.46/47, 82/83)

Digital culture

The four members of eBoy (p.48/49) operate
collectively but are geographically remote. Two
members share a studio in Berlin, another operates
from a separate studio in the same city; the
fourth is permanently based in New York. This
style of working is certainly facilitated by new
technology and the Internet but has also allowed
the group to create challenging work such as their
eCities project——a series of icon-based cities
that are constantly updated. Each city is
painstakingly built from individual elements
created in Photoshop which operate as a visual
lexicon, allowing the group to create their own
urban world of cute but disturbing images of
metropolitan life and consumption.

This work is representative of a growing digital
culture within image-making, and this book
contains examples of work from individuals
and groups such as Quickhoney (p.II, 7I, II7),
Designershock (p.60/6I, I52/I53), and Pixelhugger
(p.32/33), who appear to inhabit worlds of their own
creation: 'Hot-wired' worlds which only exist via
the Internet and the hard disk. In many cases
the work is sophisticated in its approach while
celebrating the low-resolution and pixellated icons
of the early days of computing. The aesthetics of a
time when the computer limited what could be done
has been updated and used to ironic effect.

Messy realities

This book also features work that contradicts
the trends described above——images that look
hand-drawn and, to our visually sophisticated
eye, might seem crude and naive. While not
entirely a rejection of the rational, hard-edged
aesthetic of the computer, this work is, in
many cases, a celebration of analog forms
of technology such as the photocopier, the
silkscreen, and the rubber stamp, more associated
with traditional approaches to image-making.
Indeed this work often uses computer technology as
a means of distribution and is, in some cases, a
result of a hybrid approach, which employs a
mix of old and new media in its production. It
represents a more humanistic approach——a form of
anti-mastery. This in itself is a form of mastery,
and is an attempt to escape the constraints of the
often cold, subtractive logic of the visual
communicator's role as a problem-solver. The
writer Matt Soar has described this role as
"squeezing messy realities into a clean envelope".

Visual agency

The UK-based group Neasden Control Centre (p.27,
30/3I, 64/65), was established in 2000. The studio
has worked for art galleries, publishers, and
the music industry, and has collaborated with
companies and individuals around the world
working "in all forms of visual communication".
The group blends illustration, typography,
animation, and print-based work claiming "there
are so many pigeon holes, why stay in the grid?".
Neasden's print-based editorial work is often
hand-drawn, as if torn straight from the pages of
a notebook, and is a combination of hand-rendered
typography and overlaid line drawing that has the
appearance of being photocopied. Other projects
adopt a similar visual approach although intended
for screen-based media such as a website.

>Kabeljau/Claudia Blum
Illustration for
Swiss economic
magazine Bilanz
about the downturn in
the economy

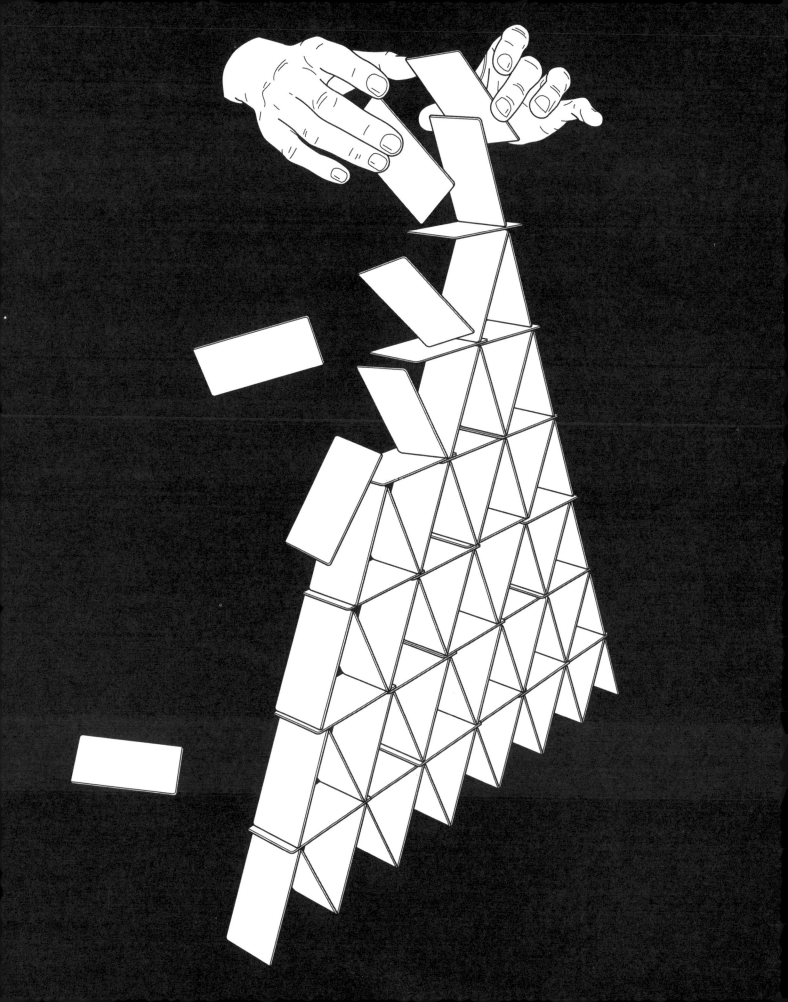

Disregarding convention

The group's own description of themselves as a visual agency is significant and indicative of a new approach where the limited titles of the past, such as illustrator or designer, are becoming increasingly redundant. This disregard for convention is also exemplified in the portfolio of work they produce—where commercial projects enjoy equal status to the self-initiated and more speculative experiments the group undertake. This continuum is described by Smith and Diamond: "Some days we are designers working in art—on others we are artists working in design".

Other individuals such as Mark Pawson (p.29, 84/85) are almost impossible to define. Pawson, who has always worked on the margins of design, illustration, and art practice, is equally disinterested in being labelled and calls himself a collector of 'stuff'. Working with rubber stamps, photocopiers, and cheap printing technology, Pawson produces work which is a celebration of the ephemeral and the everyday. Publications such as Noggins (p.84/85) are personal projects that explore his obsession with collecting and recording. Other work, which involves a process of overprinting on found materials (such as billboard posters) using the photocopier, creates a visual storehouse of imagery which, in one instance, was employed by Levi's Jeans for an advertising campaign.

The significance of the recent changes within the practice of illustration and image-making can be seen in this form of multidisciplinary approach. Groups such as MM in France continue to expand their portfolio of work through a diverse range of approaches. Currently the partnership of Michael Amazalag and Mathias Augustyniak run MM as a design practice whose work includes posters and typefaces, and videos for musicians such as Bjork. They art-direct French Vogue and have created a successful advertising campaign for Calvin Klein in the US. This approach is as much about changes within graphic design as it is about changes within the profession of illustration—much of the work featured appears to move seamlessly between the arguably outdated subsections of the profession of visual communication. While this book does not claim to offer a new and more complete title for illustration, it is an attempt to encapsulate a body of work that provides the reader with a more inclusive view of the practice of commercial image-making.

Visual research

Chapters within the book explore not only editorial, advertising, and campaign work, but also a wide range of self-generated projects which enable the reader to see the connection between the personal concerns of the illustrator operating as an author—manifest in highly individual projects, and how this is applied and extended in commercial activity.

Unseen Substance (p.40/4I), a self-initiated project produced by Jason Edwards and Tim Hutchinson of the UK design practice Bark, provides an excellent example of how this mutually beneficial relationship operates in practice. The project provides Edwards and Hutchinson with an area of visual research—an opportunity to explore ideas and to develop a new visual grammar which informs their approach to design in general.

>Yee-Haw
Letterpress Industries
Original woodcut
produced for a
self-promotional poster
2002 (p.56/57,
I56/I57, I58/I59)

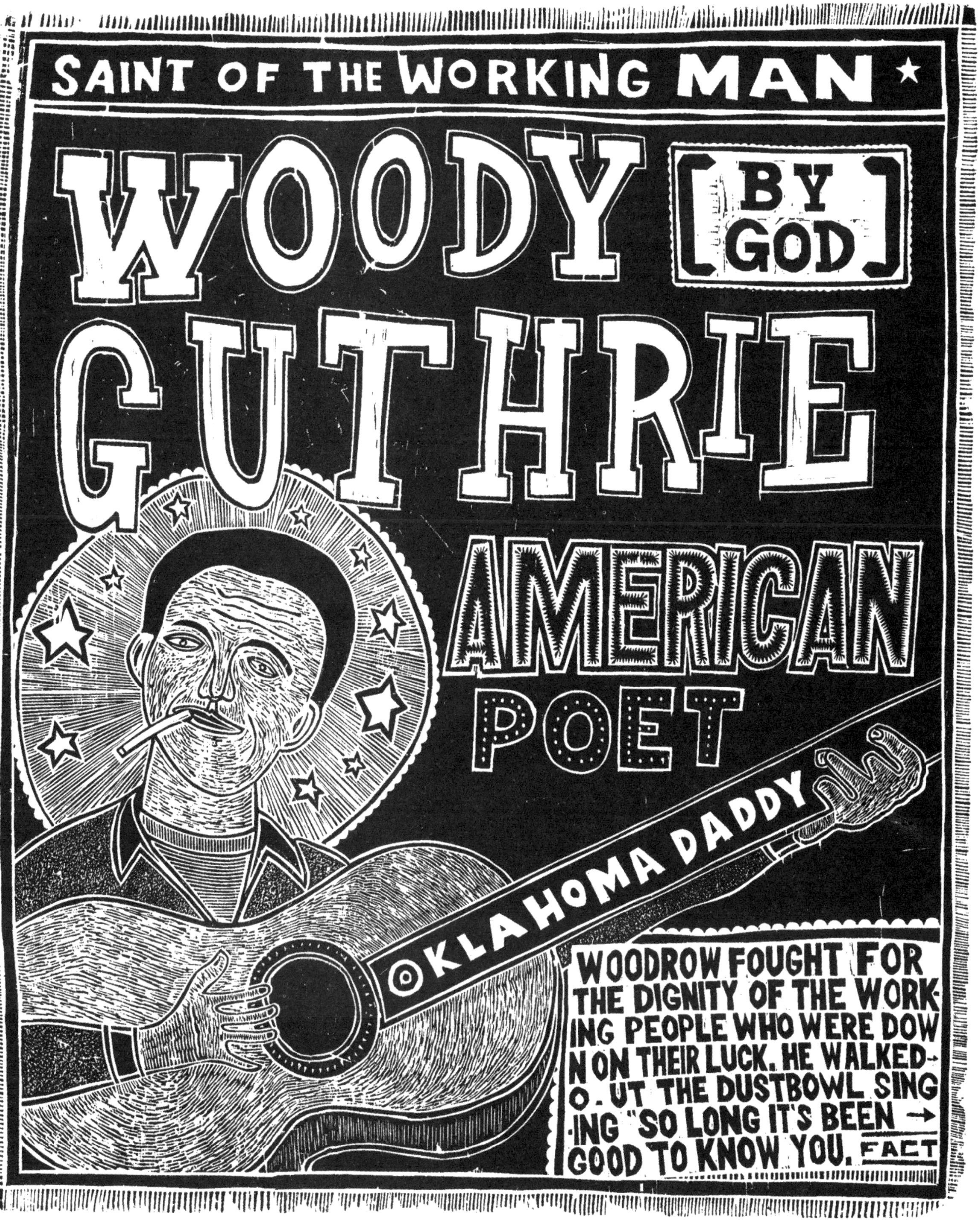
SAINT OF THE WORKING MAN
WOODY [BY GOD]
GUTHRIE
AMERICAN POET
OKLAHOMA DADDY
WOODROW FOUGHT FOR THE DIGNITY OF THE WORKING PEOPLE WHO WERE DOWN ON THEIR LUCK. HE WALKED OUT THE DUSTBOWL SINGING "SO LONG IT'S BEEN GOOD TO KNOW YOU. FACT

Unseen Substance investigates the language of
printing and packaging information most often
found on the underside of products such as milk
cartons, and uses this raw data to construct an
idiosyncratic visual language or system. This is
then applied in the construction of visual essays
and three-dimensional prototypes. The crossover to
the commercial activity undertaken by the group
can be seen in projects where they draw upon the
'findings' of their personal projects.

We are witnessing a discipline in a constant state
of transformation and flux. Certainly from within
the profession some would say it is a situation
that is well overdue. The open-ended and ongoing
nature of this transformation points to the
difficulty of arriving at a single or definitive
title for the wide-ranging nature of the activity.
While it is essential for both the illustrator
and the commissioner of illustration to have a
well-developed awareness of the contemporary
scene, its scope is not necessarily diminished
by the employment of an established and
descriptive title such as the word illustration
provides——a title which is at least widely
recognized and understood.

In interviewing individuals involved in the
practice and discipline of illustration, and in
reviewing work from around the world, my own
understanding of the nature of illustration has
been altered. I am extremely grateful to the many
people who allowed access to their work and gave so
freely of their time to assist in the production of
this book. Without this level of co-operation and
insight this project would not have been realized.

>François Chalet
Detail of illustration
from the Brazil project
(p.75, I2I)

Self-initiated & independent projects

Anthony Burrill, Neasden Control Centre, Mark Pawson, Pixelhugger, Alex Williamson, 1000 Journals, Bark, Nathan Jurevicius, Rinzen, eBoy, Gobler Toys, THS, Designershock, Grundy Northedge, Yee-Haw Letterpress Industries, Jonathan Barnbrook, Rian Hughes

Commercial illustration's rich history as an art form can be referenced to another body of work, which is equally significant and well established. This work is also illustration, self-initiated or self-generated, created by illustrators seeking to produce work outside the commercial arena and the restraints of a client brief.

This long-standing tradition of non-commercial work is mainly concerned with the notion of authorship. For others in the field of visual communication, such as graphic designers, this area of work is a very recent phenomenon which has proved to be problematic. While graphic design can be described in a similar manner to illustration—concerned with the relationship of words and images—more often the designer is working to a given content within defined boundaries such as a particular audience for the client. This does not deny the mediating role of the designer but is largely concerned with interpretation rather than origination. Self-initiated work is more common within illustration than in graphic design and as such is a more established and accepted practice.

Authorial voices

Illustration has a longer tradition of an authorial role or voice allowing individuals and groups to generate work which has informed and defined the discipline of image-making in general. Unsurprisingly for a profession which is traditionally focused upon the text and its visualization, illustrators are more than accustomed to a content-orientated approach to visual communication. This familiarity has allowed individuals to operate outside the commercial arena to build a secondary, but inter-related portfolio of work. This relationship between client-based work and personal work is mutually beneficial. The illustrator creates a range of work, some of which is used commercially and some of which is developed solely for personal interests. This latter body of work may in turn bring about new commissions.

Historically this has taken a number of forms: the illustrator both writing and creating images for projects such as children's books, or the documentation of a visit to a foreign country or city in the form of a visual travelogue, for example. This work often stands in its own right as an exhibition or publication but is also part of the development of a personal portfolio that is different to, but runs parallel to commercial activity. Often this has been a necessity—borne from a need to develop work outside of commercial restrictions, and the desire to advance individual craft and career aspirations.

Complete control

Recently the practice of self-generated work has been updated and extended by illustrators and designers who have made use of the rapid changes within the discipline of visual communication. These are not only driven by technological advances but also by a shift in perception from within the profession—concerned with the way in which illustrators and image-makers have begun to work. The traditional hierarchy of the illustrator working under the direction of the art director or commissioner has been partly overturned.

>Anthony Burrill
Yellow Flowers from a
self-initiated ongoing
project entitled Floral
Display 2003

As illustration has grown to accommodate new approaches and ways of working, it has created the opportunity for illustrators to work in a more holistic manner—as they operate a greater degree of control over the project as a whole. Small and distinctly independent groups have emerged such as Neasden Control Centre (p.30/3I, 64/65). This style of collaborative working has been developed into collective approaches to illustration, such as Beast magazine, conceived and managed by THS in Germany (p.52/53) and in the development of extended networks such as the I000 Journals project (p.36/37, 38/39) run from San Francisco by the mysteriously titled Someguy.

Work produced by both individuals and groups or collectives such as Jonathan Barnbook (p.I3, 58/59, 90/9I, 96/97), Andy Simionato (p.06, 22, 66, II4, 78/79, 80/8I), Bark (p.40/4I), THS (p.52/53), and eBoy (p.48/49), has contributed to the new relationships between commissioned and self-initiated projects. The distinct boundaries that persisted in the past have become blurred. Now the self-initiated work of these illustrators and image-makers is often the source of new commercial projects.

In many cases this work acts as a visual manifesto. Evidence of this can be seen in the upturn in the number of monographs on individual illustrators and groups recently available. These extended portfolios act as both a space in which to explore new ideas, and as a form of idiosyncratic promotion. Many of the illustrators featured in this chapter have developed an internet presence through their own websites. These websites give illustrators the opportunity to exhibit the sum total of their work and are often projects in their own right—the design and organization of the websites being as creatively significant as the work contained within.

Jonathan Barnbrook's Virus website promotes and sells his fonts, as well as advancing his approach to design in general through the visual appearance of the website itself. Animation and PDF downloads offer the opportunity to view his work in progress and to observe projects not widely published.

Many of these websites provide a series of links to other websites, revealing musical influences and personal interests, including websites of other illustrators. This network demonstrates the degree to which the work of contemporary illustration is interconnected, and at the same time self-aware. The traditional ghetto of self-generated work is reinvented through these electronic means, allowing not only new forms and approaches to emerge, but also providing some form of guarantee that the work will be seen.

This field of operation has also provided the opportunity to develop new forms of illustration, which explore not only the means of production, but also of distribution. This is a Magazine (p.78/79, 80/8I), is an electronic journal of illustration available without charge as a download from their website. Much of the work featured is self-initiated or experimental and in some cases explores the possibilities presented by the project, now in its eighth issue. The magazine behaves as if it were a print-based journal: pages turning back and forth as the reader clicks on them. It also contains animations and sound.

>Neasden Control
Centre
Self-promotional
postcard
(p.30/3I, 64/65)

Neasden

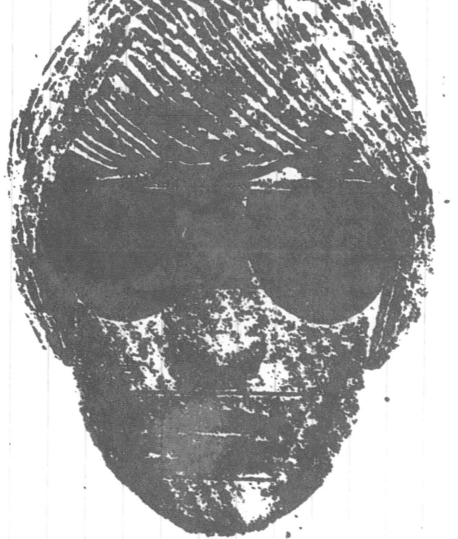

HTTP://WWW.NEASDENCONTROLCENTRE.COM
INFO@NEASDENCONTROLCENTRE.COM

METERS 2ND
NW7 16:30

RUN NUMBER: 0022425		IEL
RUN DATE:	NON-STANDARD H
OF 100	NCC
OPERATOR CODE	PRODUCT COD
RS LONDON INFORMATION 124-75	68000

In many cases the work featured in this chapter exemplifies the recent changes in the practice of illustration and the use of images within visual communication in general. The discipline has been able to build upon its established methods of working—integrating new approaches that are a result of the possibilities presented by new technology. In the process, illustration has branched out into new areas such as the internet and started to push new boundaries, naturally leading to a redefinition of the activity.

While some recent forms of illustration are more concerned with a more human and hand-drawn approach to the creation of images, others have benefitted from these interconnected and global communications. This ever-growing networked culture has established unofficial and informal links which have encouraged valuable exchanges between individuals and groups, and made an overwhelming contribution to the current vibrancy of illustration.

>Mark Pawson
Photograph of Noggins
from the self-produced
publication of the same
name (p.84/85)

^ ^ >
I. 2. 3.
Neasden Control Centre
Client: 55 DSL
Date: 2002

These images, entitled Psychodelic Military, were produced for the 55 DSL exhibition stand at the 2002 ASR Conference in San Diego in the US. The images above are from a t-shirt and label pack.

The image opposite was eventually reproduced as a large scale banner at the conference. The group produce work for a wide range of clients, as well as developing their own experimental projects.

^ > v
I. 2. 3.
Pixelhugger/Pete
Everett
Client: Pixelhugger
Date: 2002/2003

Pixelhugger began life as an experimental digital font and has grown into a website. Pete Everett creates all Pixelhugger artwork by hand, using the single pixel pencil tool in Photoshop and Director. In Everett's own words the Pixelhugger website "embraces the digital aesthetic, the humble pixel, especially with regard to typography".

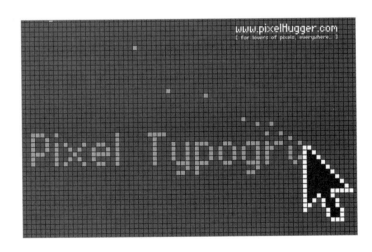

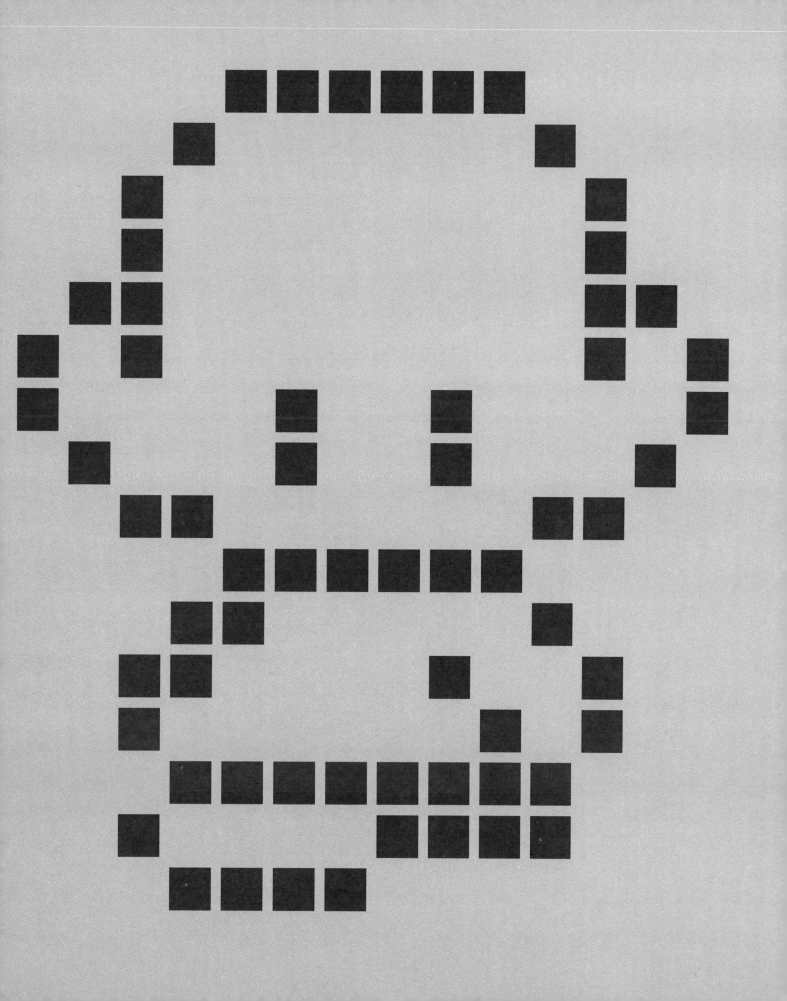

^ >
I. 2.
Alex Williamson
Client: Alex Williamson
Date: 2002/2003

These pages are reproduced from Alex Williamson's sketchbooks. They were originally created on an extended road trip across the US. Williamson often employs this method of note-taking as a form of visual research in his commercial practice. Work from this field trip was used as the basis for an exhibition at Pentagram in London. Williamson's use of a wide range of media is also reflected in his professional career, where he is as comfortable working with moving image and animation as he is with print-based editorial commissions.

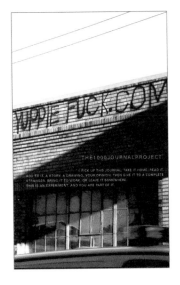

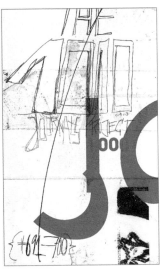

^ >
I. 2.
1000 Journals/Someguy
Client: 1000 Journals
Date: 2000

Featured here is some of the work in a completed journal returned to and reclaimed by the 1000 Journals project. The project sprang to life in 2000 when 1000 blank journals were released into the world by Someguy in San Francisco. These journals, which can be tracked on the project's own website, are contributed to and then returned to San Francisco for a big exhibition of all 1000 complete journals.

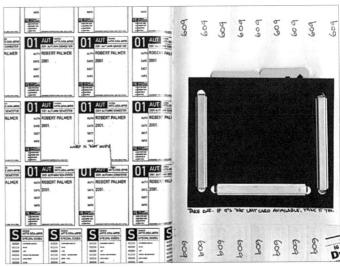

^ >
I. 2.
I000 Journals/Someguy
Client: I000 Journals
Date: 2000

Inside spreads and material from individual volumes from the I000 Journals project. The idea has its roots in the mail-art networks of the recent past but also draws upon the game of the 'Exquisite Corpse' played by the surrealists during the 1920s. The project uses the internet to build a network of collaborators around the world who in many cases may never have met but whose work is brought together in printed form.

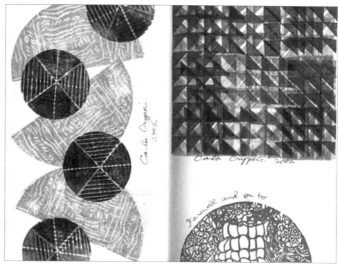

^ >
I. 2.
Jason Edwards & Tim
Hutchinson
Client: Bark
Date: 2000

This self-initiated
project entitled Unseen
Substance is an
exploration of the
printed information
found on the underside
of commercial
packaging. Bark
created systems of
classification for
these marks which
they reinterpreted in
visual essays and 3D
cartons which they
later exhibited.

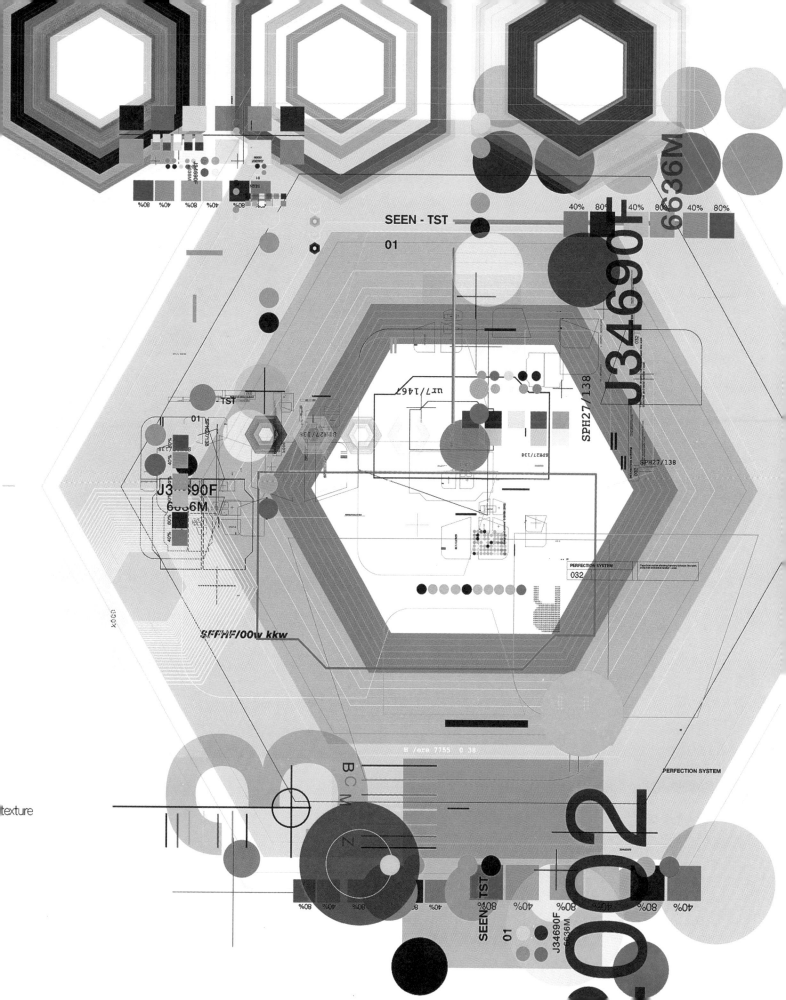

^ >
I. 2.
Nathan Jurevicius
Client: Nathan
Jurevicius
Date: 2000

Nathan Jurevicius' creation Scary Girl has slowly been developing a cult following around the world. These early drawings show the various stages of development Jurevicius went through before finally settling on the finished appearance of Scary Girl. She now has her very own online comic and advertising, as well being collected as a 3D toy.

< ^
I. 2.
Nathan Jurevicius
Client: Junkfood
Date: 2002/2003

Aside from his own
Scary Girl creation,
Nathan Jurevicius
works as a commercial
illustrator. These
early developmental
sketches and finished
pieces are for the
website of an
alternative clothing
company called
Junkfood in the US.
Online, the images are
both animated and
interactive, and
convey information
about the company and
its clothing range.

^ ^ v >
I. 2. 3. 4.
Rinzen
Client: Die Gestalten
Verlag/RMX
Date: 2003

These images are drawn from Australian-based Rinzen's own RMX project. The group, formed in 2000, produced the first version for a conference in Sydney in 200I—an audio CD of chopped-up and remixed speech and noise. Later versions involved working with an extended network of invited designers such as The Designers Republic, Future Farmers, eBoy, and Designershock; all used vector-based graphics so that images could be passed electronically between them.

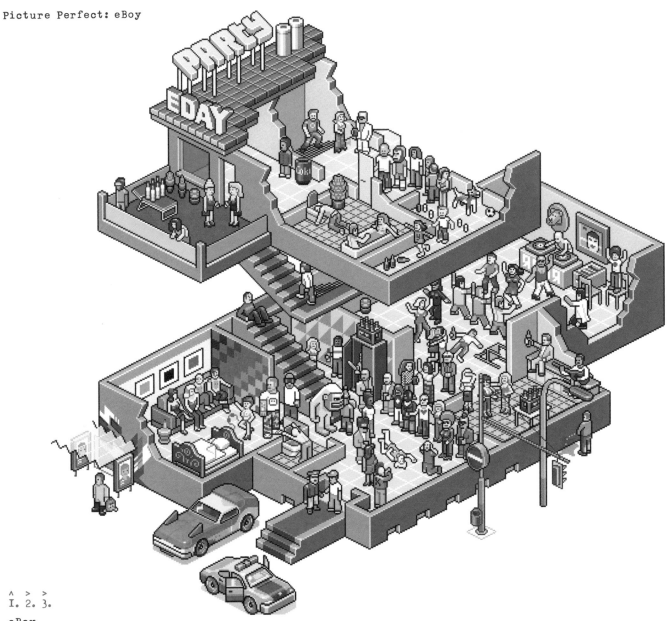

^ > >
I. 2. 3.
eBoy
Clients: Der Spiegel/
Unispiegel, The Face,
Electronic Gaming
Monthly
Date: 2002

eBoy have developed a
visual language and
world of their own.
This visual language,
created in Photoshop,
is used to create
imaginary cityscapes

and worlds; images of
metropolitan existence
that are often complex
and darkly humorous.
These editorial
illustrations
demonstrate the

popularity of their
approach: the German
publication Der Spiegel,
the Miami Winter Music
Conference, and the
Xbox game Halo.

v v >
I. 2. 3.
Steve Casino
Client: Gobler
Toys/Yumfactory
Books
Date: 1999—2003

These illustrations for the Gobler Toys website create a curious conundrum for any casual surfer who happens upon it. At first they appear to be real toys from an earlier age, but a closer inspection of the adverts and the objects themselves reveals that they are a surreal parody of a toy company. In Casino's words they demonstrate an "innocence from a bygone era". This romantic view of childhood toys belies the ludicrousness of characters such as Louie the Cheese Shark and Komrade Kluck, who make wry observations on American culture of the 1950s.

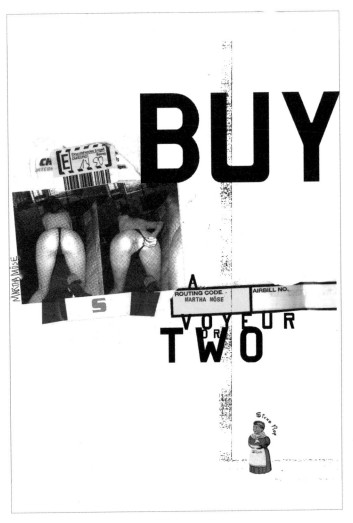

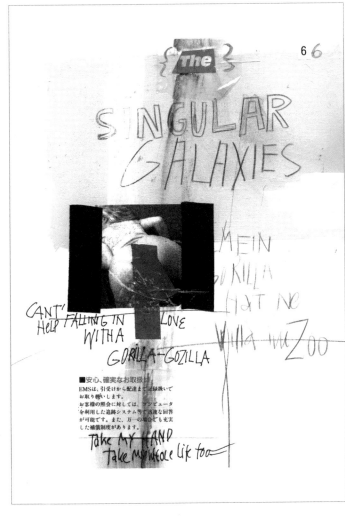

^ ^ >
I. 2. 3.
Beast
Client: THS
Date: 200I-2002

Beast magazine was produced in Germany over a period of one year. Thomas Schostok produced twelve issues which were available as free, downloadable PDF files. Described by Schostok as having "no HTML, no Flash, no content, no sponsors, no banner, and no ads", each issue was based on a theme, including Consumption, and Taste & Emotions. Designers and artists were invited to contribute to this distinctly non-commercial venture which, albeit shortlived, provides a useful example of how technology can be employed in alternative forms of publishing.

BEAST

6

THE
BIBLE
OF INSPIRATI

^ ^ >
I. 2. 3.
Peter Grundy
Client: Grundy
Northedge
Date: 2003

Peter Grundy is known for his particular approach to design and illustration which he describes as "illustration to explain rather than decorate". This very visual form of what is more often termed information design, contradicts the expectation of a discipline concerned with a clean-edged and impersonal graphic approach. These Square Heads were produced for an exhibition of Grundy's work in London in 2003.

^ ^ > > >
I. 2. 3. 4. 5.
Yee-Haw Letterpress
Industries
Client: Yee-Haw
Letterpress Industries
Date: 1997—2002

These posters, produced by Julie Belcher and Kevin Bradley, celebrate US southern culture and in particular the greats of Country and Western music, often depicting the darker side of celebrity. The Whoop-ass and Rebarant posters above are described by Belcher as "a big ole hillbilly business card".

THE FIRST FAMILY OF THE COUNTRY MUSIC

NO WE'RE NOT THE JET-SET WE'RE THE OLD CHEVROLET SET. OUR DRINK AINT MARTINIS. ITS DRAFT BEER & WEENIES.

THEY HAD A ON AGAIN, OFF AGAIN LOVE STORY. THEY BOUGHT THEIR WEDDING RING AT A PAWN SHOP IN CHICAGO. SAID THEY GONNA BUT HAD A O THEY THAT WERE HOLD ON THEY DIVORCE TRUE FACT MR

GEORGE JONES AND TAMMY WYNETTE

MEMPHIS TENNESSEE
WORLD ★ SUN RECORDS ★ FAMOUS
CARL PERKINS   JERRY LEE LEWIS
WALK THE LINE
JOHNNY CASH
RING OF FIRE
"KINGS" OF ROCK A BILLY
IN GOD WE TRUST FACT
LUTHER PERKINS — STAND UP —
IN JUSTICE HE WORE BLACK TO MARRY JUNE CARTER
MARSHALL GRANT
HE QUIT PILLS AND WHISKEY
AND THE TENNESSEE TWO
TWO MECHANICS AND A USED APPLIANCE SALESMAN
CHARLIE RICH   ELVIS PRESLEY

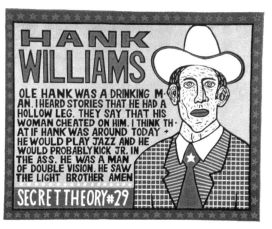

HANK WILLIAMS
OLE HANK WAS A DRINKING MAN. I HEARD STORIES THAT HE HAD A HOLLOW LEG. THEY SAY THAT HIS WOMAN CHEATED ON HIM. I THINK THAT IF HANK WAS AROUND TODAY + HE WOULD PLAY JAZZ AND HE WOULD PROBABLY KICK JR. IN THE ASS. HE WAS A MAN OF DOUBLE VISION. HE SAW THE LIGHT BROTHER AMEN
SECRET THEORY #29

< ^
I. 2.
Jonathan Barnbrook
Client: Virus Foundry
Date: 1997

The Apocalypso font, designed by Barnbrook for his own Virus Foundry, is an ironic comment on the language and spin of news reporting. The ridiculousness of phrases such as 'friendly fire' and 'nuclear winter' are exaggerated into icons that bring to mind the extent of media intrusion into our everyday lives.

^
I.

Designershock
Client: Die Gestalten
Verlag
Date: 1997

This illustration from DSOSI (Designer Shock Operating System I—The User's Manual) is an advert for the Electronic Playmate (EPM) Popporn™ (fontgame). The illustration was also used to generate the interface of this online game. With each EPM the DSOSI user is able to win and download typography. The book attempts "to defy the fixed format of conventional books". The manual offers the user a selection of the group's fonts and vector graphics which can be accessed via a CD-ROM and website. The user is required to interact by playing games to win bonus fonts and further

opportunities, and
tools to manipulate the
fonts. By blurring
the boundaries between
book, website, tool,
and user the manual
creates an unusual

symbiosis between
pixel font layouts,
screensavers,
wallpapers, and icons.

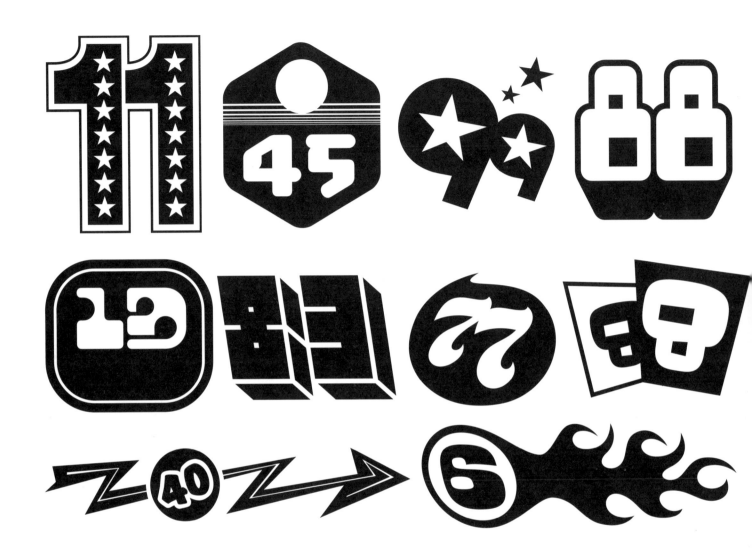

^ >
I. 2.
Rian Hughes
Client: Device
Fonts/Rian Hughes
Date: 2000

The HotRod font, drawn
by Rian Hughes for his
own foundry Device
Fonts, is based on the
numbers and decals
of custom cars and
drag racers. This
celebration of the
racing circuit is one
of many fonts produced
by Hughes over the last
few years. The fonts
form part of a uniquely
broad portfolio which
includes comics, logo
design, advertising,
and packaging.

Stephen Smith & Marcus Diamond
Neasden Control Centre, London

Formed in 2000, Neasden Control Centre is a
London-based collective. The group comprises
Stephen Smith, Marcus Diamond, Ross Holden, Matt
Ward, and a growing number of collaborators,
including musicians.

Could you tell me how you all came to work together
and where the name of the group comes from?

Unemployment led us from Brighton [on the south
coast of England] to London in 1999. Matt and Ross
joined soon after working on illustration projects
as freelancers. We did find that no feedback from
art directors at the time led to nothing. Around
that time we moved to Neasden, overlooking the
North Circular ring road and a building called
Neasden Control Centre [the Jubilee Line control
tower for the London Underground]. Self-initiated
book projects and editioned work were distributed
over the net and anywhere we could get to with a
one-day subway ticket.

You use the phrase 'visual agency' to describe
what you do. Can you explain it further and say
why it has significance for you?

A visual agency best describes our practice. We
throw all the elements together, whether graphic
or not. Art galleries are blank pages in books to be
filled. But I hate the words visual agency.

There appears to be a constant in your work which
is very recognizable, whether self-initiated or
commissioned. Could you talk about your approach?

Design groups would never employ us so we employed
ourselves. London still hasn't phoned. Unbelievable

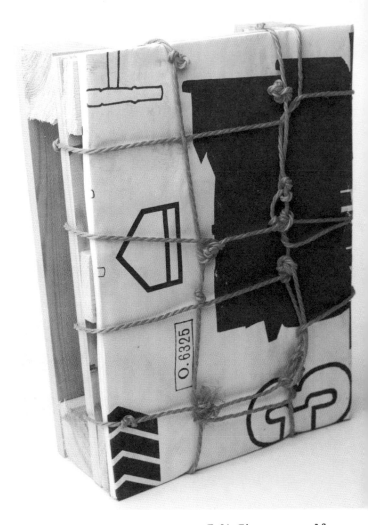

>Felt Tipper: a self-
published A4 book in an
edition of 10 released
in 2001

to think we're working for clients abroad but
without all the benefits, i.e. the weather.
Drawing, always drawing, as long as there's
drawing there's a line. Cross it and that's it.
We respond naturally to projects. Our work is in a
constant state of flux. If a comparison between
self-initiated and commissioned work is apparent
then this is due to that initial response as
illustrators. Our ethos demands we push and
experiment more and more on each new project. We
are currently redesigning Action Aid's conference
room with floor-to-ceiling digital prints,

organizing an exhibition and a series of openings for the release of our first book, designing some t-shirts for a snowboard company, and exhibiting artwork in Munich for Modart Europe 00I.

Whose work has influenced you?

I think we tend to look to artists rather than the crazy world of illustration. That doesn't mean to say we're not aware of it, it's just a lot of it isn't that interesting to us. We met with Ian Wright and Vaughan Oliver [established UK illustrators] a few times and got some positive feedback. Just looking at how others view the world is always interesting.

Editorial & publishing projects

Lawrence Zeegen, Quickhoney,
Cosmic Debris: Emily the Strange,
Oopsy Daisy, & Bon Bon, François Chalet,
Andy Simionato, Rinzen, Mark Pawson,
Alex Williamson, Jasper Goodall,
Jonathan Barnbrook, Marion Deuchars,
Arkitip, Paul Wearing, Lizzie Finn,
Ward Schumaker, Garth Walker

Traditionally the most prolific use of illustration has been in editorial design. This area is mainly concerned with printed media, such as magazine covers and articles, and book jackets. It has offered wide ranging opportunities for image-makers to produce work, which for some has provided the basis of a meaningful and singular career. Others have continued to produce work in this area but have also developed a wider portfolio that encompasses formats as varied as annual reports, record sleeves, and identity design. The use of new technology within illustration is a fairly recent phenomenon, and has allowed the exploration of alternative forms of image-making. This has not only changed the nature of how images are produced, but has also broadened and updated editorial work in general. This has had an effect on the nature of both experimental work and the mainstream. Any discussion of 'publishing' now includes areas such as website design, interactive media, animation, and moving image.

Independent approaches

Other changes, such as those within publishing, include the growth of smaller scale and independent publishing houses. These publishers have inherited the shifts in the media industry that took place during the 1980s. At that time, the significant market leaders were the new and independent magazines such as The Face and ID. This new breed of publishers, editors, and art directors included Neville Brody, Terry Jones and Ian Swift, who began to apply illustration in different ways: it was often integrated into fashion spreads, giving a unique atmosphere to the story, and affecting the overall look of a title.

Dynamic publishing

This earlier work has certainly been built upon during the last ten to fifteen years, since the arrival and subsequent wider availability of new technology. Journals such as Beast in Germany (p.52/53), I-jusi in South Africa (p.II0/III, II2/II3), Arkitip in the US (p.94/95), and This is a Magazine in Italy (p.78/79, 80/8I) have emerged in recent years. While these largely independent publications have a particular focus on illustration, graphic design, and visual culture, in many cases they present interesting models for mainstream publishing of how magazines can behave differently. Both Beast and This is a Magazine are electronic journals available freely over the internet as PDF downloads. Both are co-ordinated by illustrators and designers: Beast by Thomas Schostok and This is a Magazine by Andy Simionato and Karen Anne Donnachie. Both magazines offer the opportunity for other illustrators and designers to publish their work outside of the usual constraints of the mainstream. The only 'edges' imposed are determined by the final screen-based presentation or format and the theme of each issue such as Fashion=Fiction, and Consumption.

The now defunct Beast was produced on a monthly basis by Schostok from Essen in Germany, and ran to an eventual I2 issues. Although intended as screen-based, the magazine takes a traditional approach in its presentation with an obvious cover and sequential pages. Its content, however, is presented largely in the form of images—the thematic approach to each issue emerging as the reader travels back and forth between its electronic spreads.

>Lawrence Zeegen
Beware 02 produced for the Experiments section of www.Zeegen.com 2002 (p.76/77)

BEWARE

Simionato and Donnachie's This is a Magazine extends the approach of Schostok's Beast, with the inclusion of pages which both animate and emanate sound, as the reader clicks the mouse to turn the pages. These magazines offer image-makers an additional opportunity to work collaboratively, within a network of like-minded contributors.

Cultural language

I-jusi, produced by Garth Walker from Durban in South Africa, is a more traditional form of publishing—appearing as a printed magazine up to four times a year. Walker, who has become a familiar figure speaking at design conferences and related events around the world, describes his approach to publishing: "The magazine aims to encourage and promote South African graphic design... [it is a] commitment to developing a design language rooted in the South African experience".

Supported by sponsorship and his own design group Orange Juice, the magazine has emerged from the new South African Rainbow Nation and celebrates the vernacular of South African daily life; a form of visual communication that has grown from the street culture and traders of the reunited country. A similar approach is also to be found in the more mainstream Colors magazine, produced and owned by the clothing company Benetton. Colors has gained a reputation for its visual representation of global cultures. Both magazines have been defined by their use of images—in large part a result of a strong editorial lead provided by graphic designers: Walker for I-Jusi and the late Tibor Kalman for Colors. While the two journals share many similarities in their approach, Colors differs in its commercial imperative linked to Benetton. I-jusi has a more singular and honest agenda in its celebration of the visual life of the new South Africa.

Influence and opportunity

There has been a significant change in the perception of what illustrators are capable of, and importantly, in the kinds of commissions on offer. Equally important is the change in how illustrators are now employed: the traditional model of a commissioned illustrator working to the brief of an art director is now outdated. The degree of control offered by the advances in technology have allowed a greater degree of influence on the part of the illustrator. Recently, a substantial proportion of illustration work disappeared to graphic designers, who, as result of advances in technology, were equally able to generate images as part of their working practice. This trend appears to have been reversed. A large number of illustrators are now accomplished designers and typographers in their own right and are able to compete alongside graphic designers for complete jobs, rather than offering just one particular aspect.

Words and pictures

Central to all illustration is the relationship of images to words. This interpretation on the part of the image-maker is not simply to illustrate a given text with images of an idiosyncratic nature or a personal style: more often the illustrator is involved in developing a range of visual strategies that extend the meaning of the text.

>Quickhoney
George Bush:
illustration for
the New York Times
Magazine 2002
(p.II, II7)

This ability relies on the illustrator's awareness of the narrative structures within the material and the further unspoken possibilities of the author's words.

This way of visually expanding on the text can be explored across a series of pages, the images building in sequence to further establish the story and message. Other briefs require the illustrator to distil the essence of the text into a single space, for example, on the jacket of a novel. In such cases the image or illustration is required to function on a number of levels. The sophistication of dealing with such demands should not be underestimated. The jacket of a book operates simultaneously as a transparent representation of its content, a point of sale, packaging, and also as a form of direct advertising.

In the past book-jacket work has provided a substantial part of the image-maker's portfolio, and often this situation continues to be the case. The illustrations produced by London-based illustrator Alex Williamson for George Orwell's renowned novel 1984 (p.86/87) do more than provide images that accompany the text: they set the atmosphere and visual tone for the reader using a contemporary and relevant look to update and refresh the author's original words.

Markedly different

Marion Deuchars' book jackets for the Hispanic language publisher, Losada, in Spain (p.92/93), were commissioned by Fernando Gutierrez at Pentagram. The brief was to create a strong visual identity for both the publisher's 2000-strong back catalogue of classics, and new, forthcoming works. The covers make reference to the publisher's golden period in the 1920s, with their use of simple but striking imagery, which is sensitive to each individual book, and its theme

and content. Color is used with equal consideration across each title to provide a clear, cohesive, and recognizable look to the series as a whole.

Ian Bilbey's work on a series of book jackets for Howard Jacobson adopts a similar approach using simple flat color as the distinguishing element. Each jacket is comprised of a single, clearly drawn portrait: the jackets are obviously related to each other but in each case are also markedly different.

Strange days

A cult following has grown up around the illustration emerging from the studio of Cosmic Debris in the US. A number of characters such Emily the Strange (p.98-101), Oopsy Daisy (p.102/103), and Bon Bon, have become hugely popular with adults, teenagers, and children alike. These cute, and in the case of Emily the Strange, somewhat dark figures, occupy a world of their own making. The studio, started in 1992 by Matt Reed and Rob Reger, has generated a wealth of published material from notebooks and stickers, to books and t-shirts, to satisfy the demands of the followers of each character.

>Cosmic Debris/Yum Pop
Bon Bon Warhol
Artist:
Noel Tolentino 2003

The life of Emily the Strange began on bumper stickers and t-shirts, and has grown via a cult following from the skateboard scene to have her own notebooks, diaries, and stationery. Emily is described by her creators as "a leader, a heroine, and a link to the devil inside of all us", and exhibits all the traits of teenage angst, as well as of the outsider and social deviant—which may explain her strange attraction for so many. Oopsy Daisy is a cute but somewhat calamity-ridden character. She is messed-up and sweet at the same time—brought to life by her sayings such as "Oops I forgot to be good!", and "Oops, I can't stop saying the f-word!". Bon Bon and Ping Pong Panda, created by Yum Pop at Cosmic Debris, are aimed at a younger teen market—one the studio describes as obsessed by hyper-cuteness summed up by the half-French, half-Japanese fashionista Bon Bon.

The work of Melbourne-based Nathan Jurevicius explores a similar but somewhat darker territory. His creation Scary Girl (p.42/43, 44/45) occupies an equal level of cult interest. Scary Girl is a psychopathic-looking character with an eye patch and hook, who occupies a world more familiar to fans of Tim Burton's animated film The Nightmare Before Christmas; a world of junk food, witches, and bizarre creatures. Similar to the work of Cosmic Debris, Scary Girl appeals to children and adults alike.

The work in this chapter is influenced by a number of factors affecting contemporary design and illustration in general. A new spirit of independence appears to be at work, driven by the greater degree of control offered by new technology, and a change in the perception of the practice of illustration. This change in perception is operating from both within the discipline, among illustrators themselves, and from without—among the art directors and clients who commission illustration. While illustrators continue to operate in a traditional and commissioned mode of working, many have also developed alternative outlets built upon collective networks and the possibilities presented by technologies such as the internet.

>François Chalet
Image extract of a v-jing animation 2001
(p.21, 121)

Lawrence Zeegen, Brighton, UK

Could you tell me about your approach to
illustration and design?

I approach illustration as an image-maker to get
around the fact that I can't draw well. I employ
ideas and processes that fit the solution and aim
to subvert messages while employing a sense of
irony and wit to the final execution. I make
images because I like graphic communication and
not because I like illustration. Most illustration
is dreadful rubbish, very little is excellent.
The fact that it'scool at the moment is good if
the standards rise.

How do you go about producing your images?

I try to bring a knowledge and understanding of
print processes to the creation of my work. I build
up images with color in a similar way to how I used
screen-print process a few years ago. As part of
my working method I use found images, drawn
images, digital kit, and a black magic marker, and
work anywhere on a G4 Powerbook plugging into large
screens, using Airport and carrying around a light,
flat USB-powered scanner. I've been doing this
thing called illustration since graduating from
college in the late 1980s and see no reason to
stop now...

^ >
I. 2.
Lawrence Zeegen
Client: The Illustrated
Ape Magazine
Date: 2002

Zeegen's work has a
particular graphic
style: images, flat
color, and typography
are built up using
a combination of
drawing, scanning,
and software packages
such as Photoshop.

^ >
I. 2.
Andy Simionato
Client: This is a
Magazine
Date: 2002

The illustrations,
entitled Kiss and
Make-up, are from the
third issue of the
electronic journal This
is a Magazine. The

downloadable magazine
was started by
Simionato and his
partner Karen Ann
Donnachie from their
base in Milan. These

images are an ironic
homage to the pop
musicians of the 1970s
and 80s such as The
New York Dolls and Roxy
Music. Their instantly

recognizable profiles
are given further
iconic status when
reduced to line art.
The magazine provides
a valuable vehicle

for designers and
illustrators to
publish their work.
The creators hope to
provide an opportunity
for unknown artists,

but the magazine has
also featured more
well-known figures
such as James Victore
and Stefan Sagmeister.

^ ^ ^ >
I. 2. 3. 4.
This is a Magazine
Client: This is a
Magazine
Date: 2002

This is a Magazine is a mix of artwork, originally created in both analog and digital form, bringing together artists, photographers, graffiti artists, illustrators, and graphic designers in an unusual format, which behaves more like an exhibition than a traditional magazine. The network of contributors has now grown to include artists from all over the world, including Anthony Burrill from the UK, and Machine from Holland.

ISSN 1721-4904

^ >
I. 2.
Rinzen
Client: Die Gestalten
Verlag/RMX
Inspired
Date: 2003

The Australian group Rinzen produced these illustrations for the Berlin publisher Die Gestalten Verlag. The illustration above is a contribution made by Rinzen for the book Brazil Inspired curated by Nando Costa. The image opposite is from Rinzen's own publication, RMX Extended Play. The book is based on thematic images created by the group, which were then passed from contributor to contributor, who were asked to 're-mix' the originals. The project explores the nature of collaboration and relies on an extended global network of contacts who work in a wide variety of disciplines from digital animation to print.

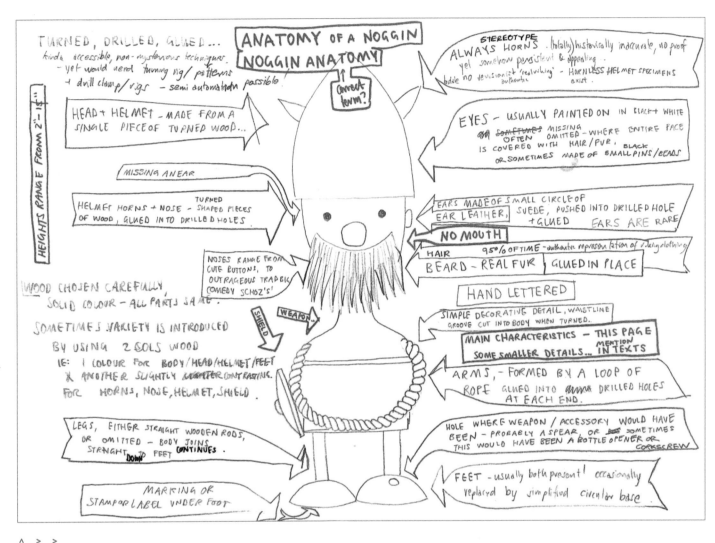

I. 2. 3.

Mark Pawson
Client: Mark Pawson
Date: 2002

Mark Pawson's name has become synonymous with small-scale and independent publishing projects, such as the Plug Wiring Diagram book and Mark's Book of Kinder Eggs. Pawson has an obsessive interest in overlooked everyday items and ephemera, exemplified in his publication entitled Noggins. Noggins details his collection of wooden Viking toys and ornaments, amassed over a number of years, and contains a detailed analysis of his collection to date. 'Low' technology plays an important part in the reproduction of these examples, as with the majority of Pawson's work.

MARK PAWSON

NOGGINS+

^ ^ >
I. 2. 3.
Alex Williamson
Client: XX Books
Date: 200I
Format: Silk-screen

These illustrations, produced for a re-issued version of George Orwell's seminal novel I984, show the breadth of Alex Williamson's work. The images were produced using silk-screen printing to provide a contemporary feel; also to fit in with the narrative which speaks of isolation and observation by an unseen and controlling 'Big Brother'. Williamson is representative of a new breed of illustrators who practice their craft across a broad range of media. He is equally happy working with printed illustration as he is producing title sequences and animations for television and the music industry.

^ ^ ^ ^
I. 2. 3. 4.

^ ^ ^ ^ >
5. 6. 7. 8. 9.

Jasper Goodall
Client: The Face
Date: 200I—2003

Jasper Goodall's distinctive style of image-making was employed by fashion and lifestyle magazine, The Face, to illustrate its editorial on trends for the coming year. The illustrations entitled Xpensive (I), Pirate (2), Petrol heads (3), Gender merging (4), Zombie (5), DIY (6), Drug bubble (7), Commune (8), and Burlesque (9), explore various trends such as lifestyle, fashion, and film which, more often than not, reveal a darker side to life. Goodall plays with the idea of zombie movies to illustrate this editorial which could be considered a comment on the slavish nature of trend followers.

^ ^ >
I. 2. 3.
Jonathan Barnbrook
Client: Booth-Clibborn
Editions
Date: 2000

This design for the book Why 2K—Anthology for a New Era, explores a series of essays on the new century. It was commissioned by the UK's Millennium Experience and includes essays by poet Seamus Heaney, and film-maker Derek Jarman. Barnbrook's use of manipulated imagery, originally drawn from photo libraries, is combined with typography that provides a visual counterpoint to the essays' content. As well as outstanding typography Barnbrook has produced a number of book designs, among them his award-winning collaboration with UK artist Damien Hirst.

You Are Here

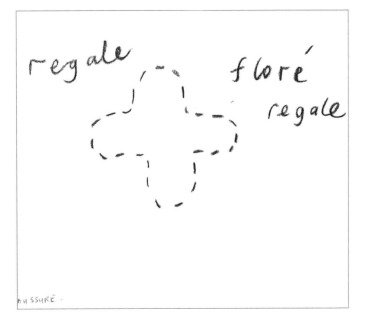

^ ^ > > >
I. 2. 3. 4. 5.

> > > >
6. 7. 8. 9.
Marion Deuchars and
Fernando Gutierrez,
Pentagram
Client: Losada
Date: 2002

This series of book covers for the Hispanic language publisher Losada creates a strong visual identity for both the company and its back catalogue of 2000 books. Although Deuchars' illustrations make reference to Losada's golden period during the 1920s, the use of simple but striking imagery and a strong color palette results in a very contemporary appeal. Each cover is treated with sensitivity to the subject matter but also retains its identity as part of a series.

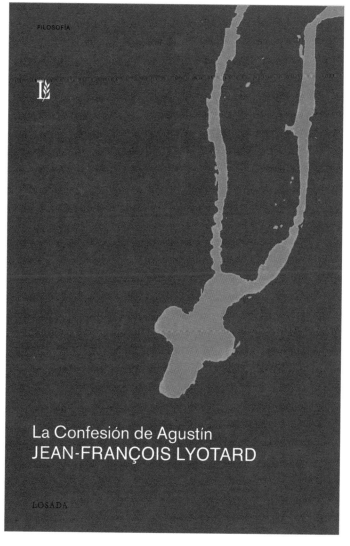

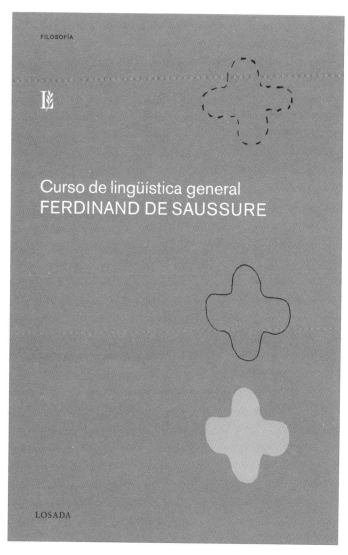

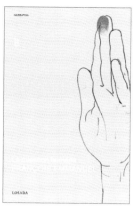

^ ^ ^ ^ ^ >
I. 2. 3. 4. 5. 6.
Arkitip
Client: Arkitip
Date: various

The Los Angeles-based Arkitip magazine is a bi-monthly publication which offers artists and designers the opportunity to create what its owners describe as "site-specific art editions".

The limited-edition magazine is numbered and stamped, and is intended to behave as if it were a group exhibition. Arkitip, which is produced in a different size and shape each month,

offers collectable editions at a reasonable price. Featured here are covers, inside pages, and exhibition posters.

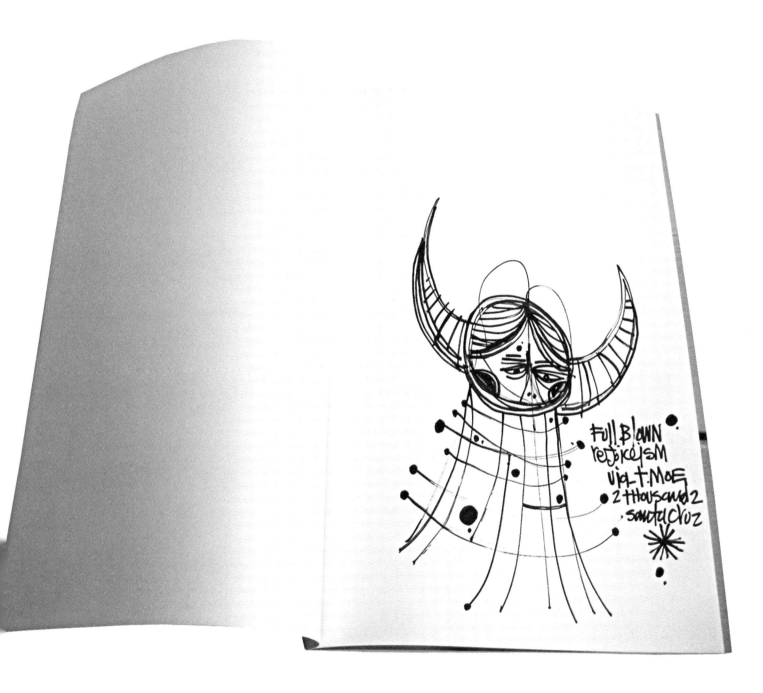

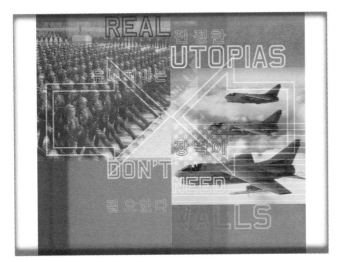

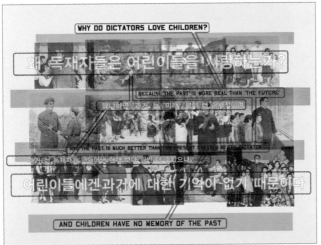

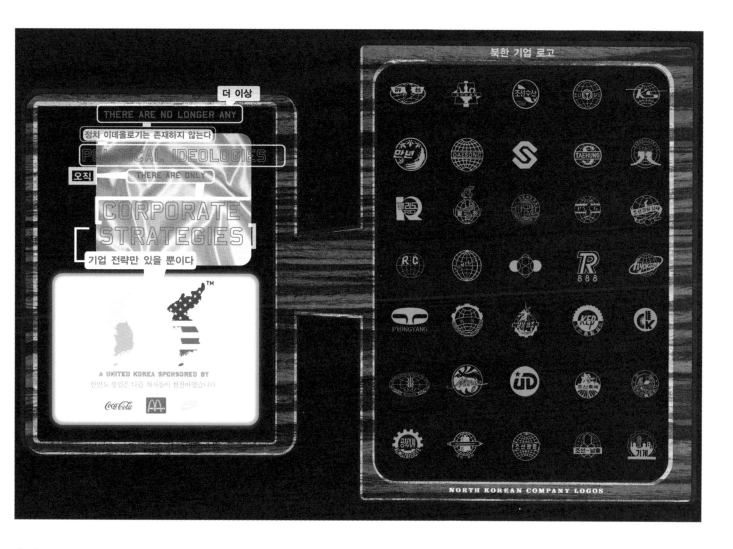

< ^
I. 2.
Jonathan Barnbrook
Client: South Korean
Magazine
Date: 200I

These spreads are from a feature created by Jonathan Barnbrook that attempts to raise issues surrounding the dictatorship which governs North Korea. The visual essay criticizes the regime, and uses the editorial space to explore ideas about freedom, and the power of the individual over totalitarian dynasties such those which have dominated North Korea.

Emily hears everything...

^ ^ > v >
I. 2. 3. 4. 5.
Emily the Strange
Client: Cosmic Debris
Artists: Buzz Parker,
Brian Brooks, Rob Reger
Date: 200I

The US-based Cosmic Debris have been responsible for creating a number of characters which have developed a cult following. Chief among the ever-growing list of characters such as Oopsy Daisy, Bon Bon, and Ping Pong Panda, is Emily the Strange, featured here and on the previous pages. From her early appearances as bumper stickers (which were appropriated by the skateboard scene) Emily has grown into a merchandise queen with her own books, posters, diaries, and so on. Part of Emily's attraction lies in her 'outsiderness' and a distinctly dark visual tone. "Emily hears everything and listens to nothing", say her creators.

...and listens to nothing.

^ ^ >
I. 2. 3.
Oopsy Daisy
Client: Cosmic Debris
Artist: Brian Brooks
Date: 2002

The character Oopsy
Daisy, created by
Cosmic Debris and
Brian Charles Brooks,
has become another of
the group's successful
projects, again
attracting a cult
following among
teenagers and adults
alike. Cosmic Debris
have taken the common
catchphrase 'Oops a
daisy', and twisted it
into more adult phrases
such as, "Oops, I got
dead", and "Oops I
killed a ninja".

^ ^ >
I. 2. 3.
Paul Wearing
Client: Random House
Vintage Classics
Date: 1998

The publishing firm
Random House
commissioned Paul
Wearing to produce
these illustrations for
a repackaging of their
classic series. The
brief asked Wearing to
produce images which
would attract a
younger and broader
audience. Wearing
approached the project
by creating images that
evoked the general
themes of Joyce's
works, rather than a
literal interpretation
of the text and the
period in which the
novels were written.

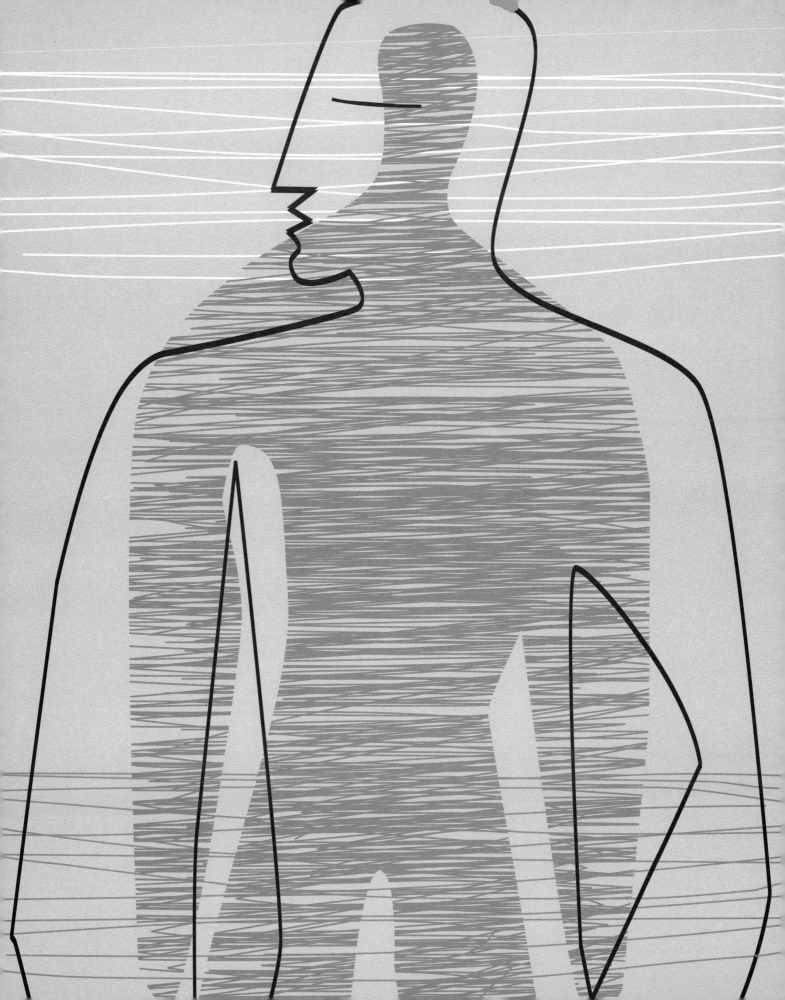

THINGS TO M

PATCHWORK

CLEVER CRAFTS

BEAGLE AMERICA

OOK

Handicrafts

Golden

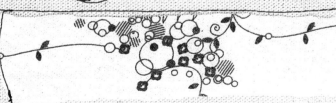

<
I.
Lizzie Finn
Client: I. Relax
magazine
Date: 2002

This image, created by
Lizzie Finn, was
commissioned by Relax
magazine, based in
Tokyo, Japan, for a
regular feature
entitled Sit Back,
Relax and Enjoy. Each
issue an invited artist
or designer is asked to
contribute an image or
illustration. Taking
the theme of craft
and embroidery, a
signifcant aspect of
her own style of work,
Finn created an image
by scanning the spines
of books, which were
subsequently
manipulated in
Photoshop, then printed
out, traced, and sewn
on to the fabric.

^ ^ > >
I. 2. 3. 4.
Ward Schumaker
Client: Yolly Bolly
Press
Date: 2000

These illustrations were produced using Letterpress by San Francisco-based illustrator Ward Schumaker. The limited edition publication of Paris France, by Gertrude Stein, gave Schumaker the opportunity to explore the relationship between traditional and new technologies, combining Photoshop with letterpress printing. Schumaker describes his approach as like "pulling potatoes from the earth: with eyes closed and fingers grasping".

PICASSO

SYLVIA BEACH

MISS MARS

ETTA CONE

LADY OTTOLINE MORREL

ANTHEIL MATISSE

GENTHE

JANE HEAP PAUL BOWLES

BRAQUE

CEZANNE

MAN RAY BERTRAND RUSSELL

JUAN GRIS

MABEL DODGE

ROGER FRY

COCTEAU

EZRA POUND

rue

APOLLINAIRE MISS SQUIRES

DERAIN EDITH SITWELL VAN VECHTEN

MAILLOL

JOHN REED

HEMINGWAY ERIK SATIE TCHELITCHEV

T. S. ELIOT PASCIN NATALIE BARNEY

BONNARD PICABIA BLAISE CENDRARS

VUILLARD DEMUTH MARINETTI

ROUSSEAU MINA LOY

BERNARD FAŸ LEO STEIN MARSDEN HARTLEY

MARIE LAURENCIN FORD MADOX FORD

WM JAMES DELAUNAY

SHERWOOD LYTTON STRACHEY

ANDERSON KAHNWEILER

EVELYN THAW FITZGERALD

MILDRED ALDRICH CLIVE BELL

MAX JACOB McALMON

PABLO CASALS

ISADORA DUNCAN

ANDRE SALMON

ANDRE GIDE

VIRGIL THOMPSON

de

FLEURUS

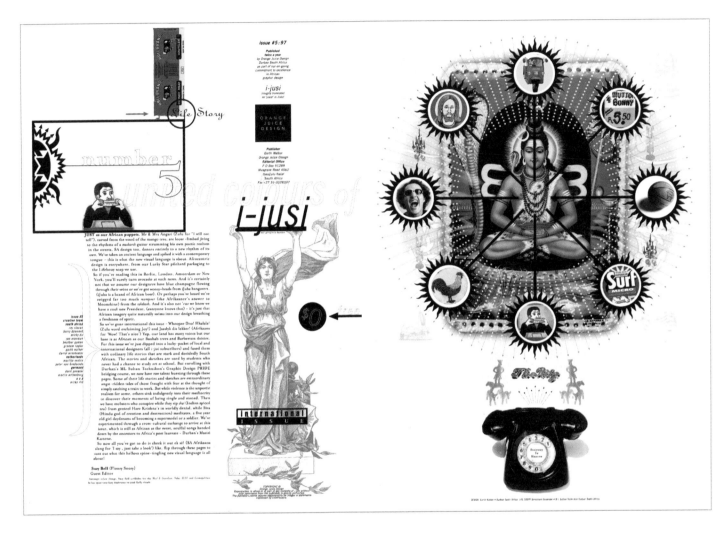

^ > > >
I. 2. 3. 4. 5.
Garth Walker
Client: I-jusi
Date: 1997

The I-jusi spreads and front covers featured here demonstrate the diversity of material in the magazine, from Street happenings to Zulu culture, and pornography/typography to sheep's heads as a delicacy. From I-jusi I4, the A-Z Issue.

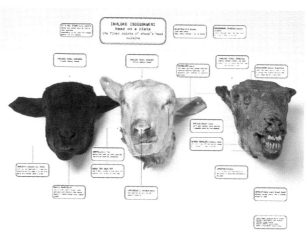

Garth Walker, I-jusi magazine
Durban, South Africa

Could you tell me about the background to the
I-jusi project, and how the name came about?

I-jusi roughly translates as "juice" in Zulu. It's
an experimental graphic design magazine which we
[Orange Juice Design] publish between two and four
times a year. The magazine aims to encourage and
promote South African graphic design. It's part of
our commitment to developing a design language
rooted in the South African experience. Designers,
illustrators, photographers, and writers, are
encouraged to create in total freedom and explore
their personal views on life in a free and
democratic South Africa.

How do you fund and produce the project?

The magazine is strictly non-commercial. Each
issue is 16 pages long, A3 in size, and is published
in a limited print run of 500-ish copies per issue.
In the spirit of ubuntu [we exist relative to one
another], the I-jusi team all contribute for free.
There is no budget for production, or anything
else! The paper is donated by South African paper
giant SAPPI, and the repro and print is done by
Orange Juice's primary supplier, The Fishwicks
Group, who reproduce all our commercial work.
Orange Juice picks up other costs such as mailing.

How do you decide on the content of each issue?

That's left up to the contributors. Each issue
is themed, which people are free to interpret
as they like. As publishers, we'd like to be far
more progressive on content and South African
historical issues but need to be sensitive to the
wishes of our co-sponsors. Ironically, and despite
our history, we enjoy a freer interpretation of
political correctness than many first-world
societies. A lesson in there somewhere...

The initiative behind I-jusi is concerned with the
notion of freedom; it is obviously important to
you, and I would imagine, all South Africans. How
does South African graphic design and illustration
relate to the recent history of your country?

The elections in May 1994 didn't just mark the
crossover into a new South Africa; they heralded a
new way of seeing. From that day on we started to
look at society and our nation differently. We had
the freedom to redefine ourselves, to feel renewed
in the present, and revitalized in the future.
From that day we all had the power, and with that
power has come a new sense of responsibility,
at least with those of us who have become
increasingly aware of the intimate connection
between the individual and society. For every
personal action there is a communal reaction, and
vice versa. These actions are described in a new
language, a visual language that everybody can
understand. One that mixes icons from the past,
and borrows from different cultures, and blends it
all together. A visual language that starts on the
streets and ends up in glossy magazines on coffee
tables. Our visual language is our most powerful
weapon—it's our tool of change. We like to think
of it as design power. The power of the creative
juices now they have been allowed to flow freely in
a new South Africa; a revolution of the power of
graphic design to promote change.

By the early 1990s the legacy of apartheid had
created an environment totally unsuited to the
sudden influx of people into the city centres and
townships. Millions lacked employment skills, many
were illiterate, and were totally unprepared for
what they found. As most were forced to live and
work anywhere and however they could, many simply
squatted on the sidewalks. Living in shacks made
from scavenged material, they began to serve the
passing trade. Overnight, shoe repairers, personal
grooming suppliers, hair salons, and general
traders sprang up on every sidewalk.

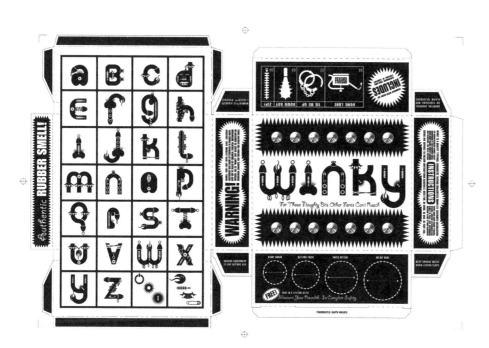

>Font based on
pornographic imagery
from I-jusi I5,
the porn issue

Market forces and competition resulted in many
traders having to advertise their wares or
services. Suddenly hand-painted signs, murals,
and hoardings began to appear. Specialist service
industries sprang up to serve these street
traders. Sign-makers began to specialize in, say,
men's barber salon signs, painted onto fabric for
portability. Many traders and their customers are
illiterate, so signage tends to be highly visual
and creative in its use of language.

Street graphics are common throughout Africa and
street graphic design is becoming increasingly
sophisticated. The medium is transient; so much
of the street vernacular is lost soon after it
has been produced. It literally serves the trader
as long as he or she trades. South Africans
are fanatically capitalist. Many traders begin

the long climb to success on the streets or
flea-markets of our cities. Graphic design is
already an integral part of that process. Their
success is design's success.

Advertising & promotional projects

Quickhoney, Future Farmers, François Chalet, Marion Deuchars, Ian Bilbey, Shepard Fairey, Grundy Northedge, Simon Emery, Frost Design, Carter Wong Tomlin, Lizzie Finn, Paul Bowman, Designershock, Rian Hughes, Yeehaw Letterpress Industries

In recent years contemporary culture has become increasingly dominated by visual communication, and in particular, commercial images. Visual communication pervades our existence through technologies such as television and the internet. The dynamic, seductive, and at times shocking visual messages can seem inescapable as they seek out their intended audiences. The strategies employed to market individual products or to emphasize a brand or a company's identity have become increasingly sophisticated, and in some cases adopt an unfamiliar level of subtlety in their use of images and illustration. This has become a necessary part of the process of selling, as the intended audience has become more visually discerning. The ubiquitous culture of the image has had an effect on both screen-based and printed media, and has encouraged a renaissance in the role and use of images within design.

Knowledge assurance

The work of illustrators such as Ian Bilbey (p.124/125, 126/127) and Simon Emery (136/137, 138/139) aids the presentation of complex information such as a company's financial position within their annual report. This activity is concerned with more than just providing pretty pictures to accompany business figures. These illustrators use their ability to visualize the world to represent information in a manner that can be easily understood.

This form of illustration represents a particular sector of the discipline—one which is more concerned with an enhanced form of representation than a direct interpretation. To operate with any degree of success, the illustrator working in this field must not only understand the information they are working with, but also the perceived values and identity that a company or product stands for. This also requires an understanding

of the particular audience the client wishes to reach, and an ability to translate this into an appropriate and effective visual language.

This does not mean that the work reduces the meaning of what it represents; what is known in graphic design as 'problem-solving' can result in a rich and diverse range of visual outcomes. Often the illustrator is employed because their style of work is, to a large degree, visually in tune with the client or product's intended audience. At other times, illustrators are contracted to enrich the client's message and extend its communication, desirability, or authority through their ability to produce a variety of styles.

Visual explanations

The work of Grundy Northedge could be regarded as information design—a discipline the group describes as "illustration to explain rather than decorate". In a series of pictograms produced for the oil company Shell International (p.134/135) they developed an icon-based system that was employed across a range of material including book dividers, posters, and even Christmas cards. The pictograms have their roots in the clean and hard-edged language of international picture symbols such as the instantly recognizable figures more often seen in signage systems.

>Quickhoney
Illustration of Madonna
for Spex magazine,
Germany 2002 (p.11, 71)

These are enlivened by a playful and humanistic approach adopted by the group. The recurring male figure is depicted in a number of attitudes which ape these signs of authority and instruction but which, on closer inspection, are subtly altered to address the message of the client; thus the pictograms are presented in a personal manner with which the audience can identify.

All dressed up

The design practice Carter Wong Tomlin were asked to develop a campaign for the clothing company Howies (p.142/143)—a company already well-known for their unusual approach to marketing. A brief was developed that involved commissioning a large number of illustrators to decorate second-hand wardrobes with messages of their own choosing. The group of illustrators, including Ian Wright, Marion Deuchars, and Andrew Mocket, produced a range of highly individual pieces of work that collectively offer an arresting visual identity and point of sale for the company.

Ian Bilbey produced a clearly recognizable identity for the clothing company, Paul Smith (p.124/125), through his clever use of images that adopt an almost retro style of illustration. Bilbey's strong visual identity is both instantly recognizable and extends the image of the business, demonstrating how illustration can be effectively used to update and extend the perception of a company or product. The Paul Smith group is more usually identified by the handwritten signature of the designer himself. Bilbey's approach to the project builds upon the quirkiness of the founder's personal signature, which has remained a constant throughout the marketing of his clothing range over the years.

Simon Emery's illustration has been used in a similar way to that of Ian Bilbey's: particularly to visualize financial data within company reports. Bilbey's illustration for the Waitrose supermarket group (p.126/127) enlivens the practical information the company needs to communicate. Emery's work for Range Rover (p.138/139) develops a visual language based upon familiar transport signs. These feature in a global map which incorporates images of rough terrain associated with Range Rover's reputation for producing hardy vehicles which can traverse rugged landscapes.

The illustrator Marion Deuchars has worked with Frost Design on a number of projects. Her illustration for the Design and Art Directors' Association's (D&AD) 2002 annual review (p.122/123) finds an unlikely solution to the presentation of figures and charts. In her now familiar drawing style, Deuchars hand-drew the information, even using the ring left behind by a coffee cup as the basis for a series of pie-charts. This approach is carried over into the typography of the report, which is entirely hand-rendered by Deuchars in pencil. The end result is an unexpected visual presentation for the association's annual report and 40th anniversary. The association, which organizes an annual competition, awards ceremony, and education program, for both the professional creative industry and students, are closely associated with the pencil. This symbol, which forms a large part of their identity, is also a three dimensional award much coveted by entrants of the annual competition.

>Future Farmers
Exhibition logo for
Wataiko Institute for
Technology (p.132/133,
148/149)

Pentagram's Angus Hyland commissioned Deuchars to produce a poster for the British Council's touring exhibition Picture This (p.146/147). The exhibition, destined for South America, celebrated contemporary British illustration. The poster was hung in art institutions and colleges to promote the exhibition and plays with the clichés of Britishness. Deuchars' approach was to play up the unusualness of typically British images when placed in a South American setting. The poster was constructed by Angus Hyland using a number of ad hoc drawings by Deuchars.

The German design group Designershock use a novel approach in their campaign and identity for the design recruitment agency Designer Dock (p.152/153). The identity is a witty take on the notion of travel and the idea of destination and arrival that exploits the ephemera of airline travel. Using a strategy that has its roots in the concept of détournement (originally proposed by the French situationists), everyday or familiar items are subtly altered to change their meaning or context.

The use of illustration to sell, persuade, or inform, provides a good example of its power to communicate beyond the level of, for instance, a photograph—adding a level of sophistication and interpretation beyond that which is achievable through the lens.

In many cases the work in this chapter is a celebration of drawing and the 'hand'. While there is a renaissance and renewed interest in illustration of a hand-drawn nature, this does not necessarily mean that a pencil is the only tool employed. The work is also concerned with other forms of drawing: using the mouse, working in three dimensions, or with the moving image, for example. The hand-drawn image which uses a particular quality of line and mark-making is

often a result of a hybrid approach to illustration. These apparently direct methods of creating images are often a result of a layering of processes. This collaging together of old and new does at times appear to be at odds with some of the harder-edged and cleaner styles of current illustration, and, although a product of new technology, it does appear, to some degree, to be a reaction to this.

>Francois Chalet
Illustration from the
Tourist project 2002
(p.21, 75)

D&AD FROM OUR ACCOUNTANT'S POINT OF VIEW

The organisation's surplus for the year was £120k. This was £29k down on the £149k achieved last year. Although sponsorships and awards entries were at record levels, Education Council funding was down on 2000, the costs of staging the awards ceremony were up by 10%, an extra 25% was spent on educational programmes and the charity's portfolio of investments fell by £20k in line with the global decline of stock market values.

Educational programmes accounted for 42% of D&AD's expenditure whilst 36% was spent on running the professional awards scheme and ceremony. 60% of the organisation's income came from entries from the professional awards scheme and sponsorships and ticket sales for the awards ceremony.

At 31 July 2001 D&AD's reserves stood at £1m. A further £150,000 was invested into the portfolio of stocks and shares in March 2001. However, the events of 11 September and the general slowdown in the global economy have meant that the charity has had to reassess strategies towards the organisation of some events and programmes occurring in 2002.

48

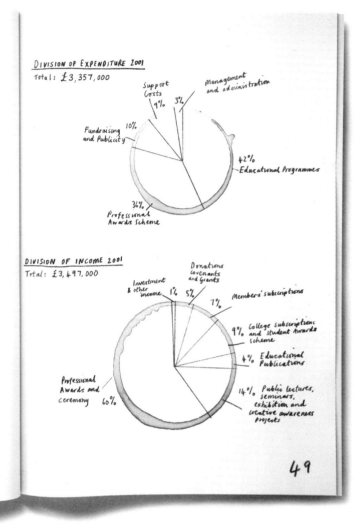

DIVISION OF EXPENDITURE 2001
Total: £3,357,000

- Support Costs 9%
- Management and administration 3%
- Fundraising and Publicity 10%
- Educational Programmes 42%
- Professional Awards Scheme 36%

DIVISION OF INCOME 2001
Total: £3,497,000

- Investment & other income 1%
- Donations covenants and grants 5%
- Members' subscriptions 7%
- College subscriptions and student awards scheme 9%
- Educational Publications 4%
- Public lectures, seminars, exhibition and creative awareness projects 14%
- Professional Awards and ceremony 60%

49

<
I. 2.
Marion Deuchars
Client: D&AD Annual
Report
Date: 2002

To mark the D&AD's 40th Anniversary, the 2002 Annual Review was given special treatment by art director Vince Frost and illustrator Marion Deuchars: all 5496 words of the text were handwritten in pencil. Using a pencil, without relying on typesetting, was an attempt to represent the organization's famous identity, which was extended with informal treatments of financial information using coffee rings for pie-charts and hand-drawn tables.

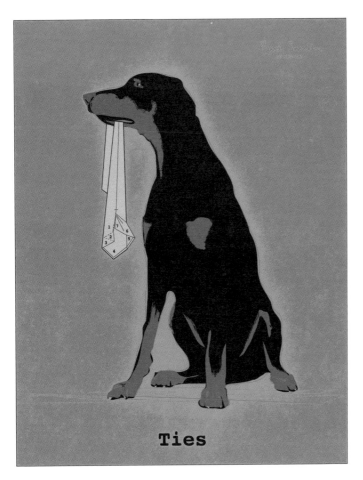

Ties

^ ^ >
I. 2. 3.
Ian Bilbey
Client: Paul Smith,
Japan
Date: 2000

Ian Bilbey was commissioned to produce a series of images to promote the Paul Smith company's Autumn/Winter collection. He was given simple one-word briefs such as belt, hat, typewriter, etc. Bilbey, who describes his method of working as "drawing with a mouse", produced these illustrations which adopt an almost retro feel. The final pieces were AI/AO in size, and are an attempt, Bilbey says "to keep it simple".

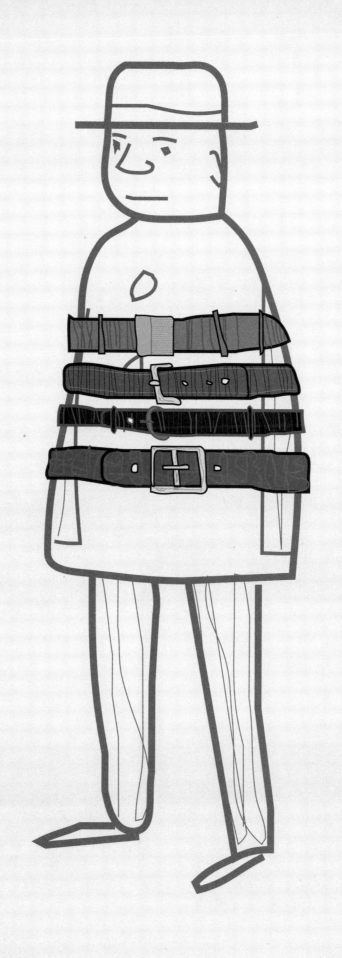

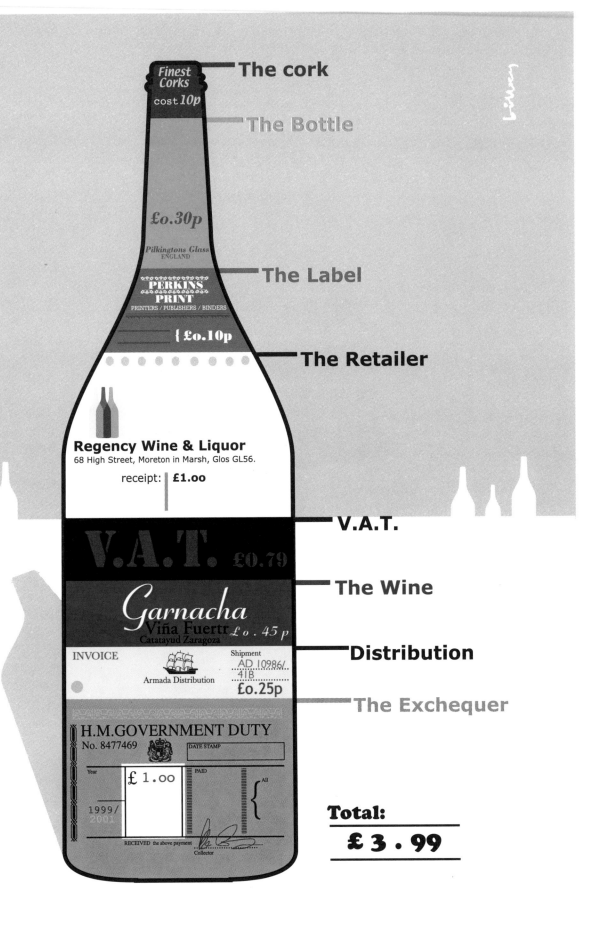

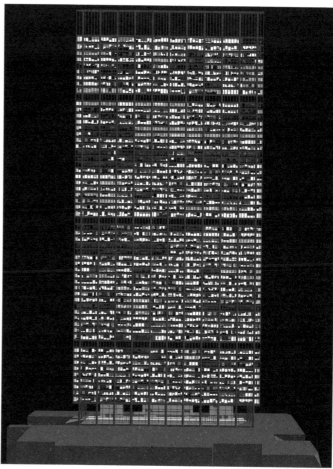

< ^ ^
I. 2. 3.
Ian Bilbey
Client: Waitrose, Kiehls
www.artifact.com
Date: 200I

These images, produced for a variety of clients, demonstrate the diversity of Ian Bilbey's approach to image-making. The image opposite, produced for the Waitrose supermarket group, visually explains how the price the customer pays for wine is reached, and could be described as a form of information design. The images above were commissions which were never published. The Chase Manhattan (Day/Night) image was originally produced for a website selling prints, and the Kiehls image was produced for a shop in New York.

^ ^ >
I. 2. 3.
Shepard Fairey
Client: Obey
Date: 2003

These limited-edition prints, produced by Shepard Fairey, are part of a larger body of work produced over the last decade more widely known as the Obey the Giant or Andre the Giant project. The images here and overleaf play with Fairey's approach to reproducing work: a form of détournement of existing images and icons. Here he appropriates punk icons Joey Ramone, Johnny Rotten, and Joe Strummer, by the addition of the one-word instruction 'Obey'. The Obey the Giant project, which began in 1989, has grown via a vast international network of collaborators who replicate Fairey's original Obey artwork.

^ >
I. 2.
Shepard Fairey
Client: Obey the Giant
Date: 2003

Here Jamie Reid's original Sex Pistols artwork is subtly altered by Shepard Fairey. The bus destinations have been changed from the original 'Boredom' and 'Nowhere' to 'No' and 'Order'. The image above is a sticker from the Andre the Giant/ Obey the Giant project.

Picture Perfect: Future Farmers

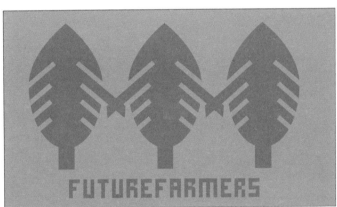

^ < ^ ^ >
I. 2. 3. 4. 5.
Future Farmers
Self-promotional logos
& poster for Design
Triennial
Date: 2002/2003

The ironic 'we never
sleep' owl logo has
become a Future
Farmers motto. This is
used by the group
(founded by Amy
Franceschini in I995)
alongside the Tree logo.
The seedling logo was
developed as part of
the group's Seedling
Toy series. The
teardrop logo was
produced for a water
purification unit
project. The poster
opposite was produced
for the US National
Design Triennial at the
the Cooper Hewitt
museum in New York,
and is intended to

promote a prototype
called Backpack
Theater Chairs.
These chairs can be
re-assembled to make
a tent, theater, bench,
or projector.

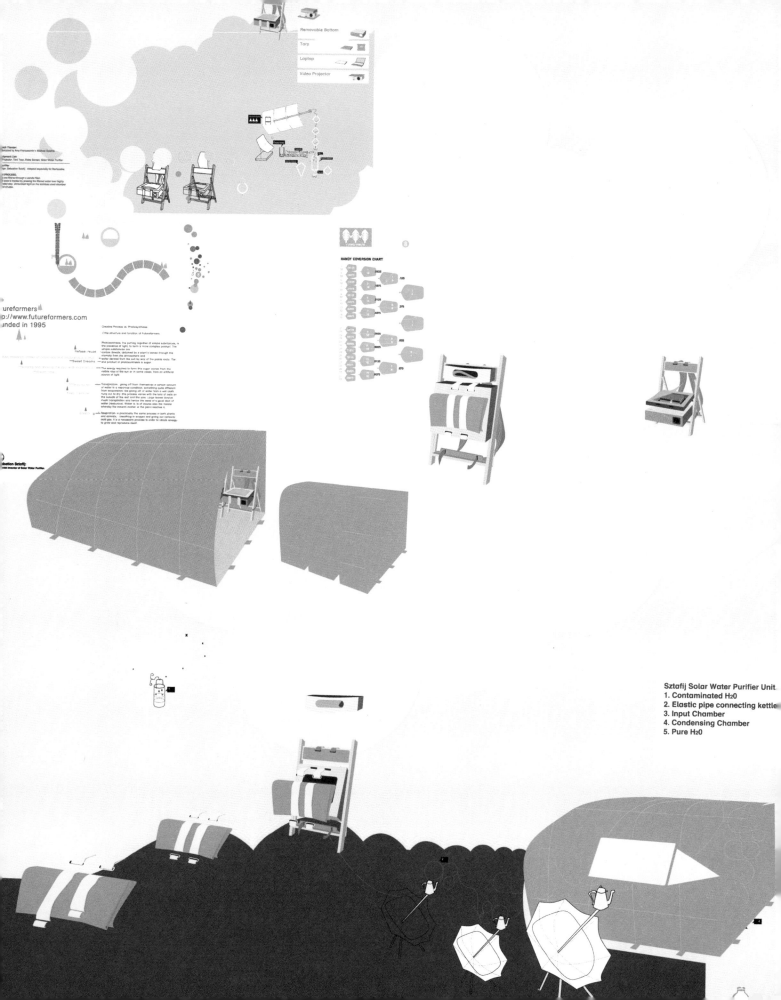

Removable Bottom

Tarp

Laptop

Video Projector

HANDY COVERSION CHART

urefarmers
p://www.futurefarmers.com
unded in 1995

Creative Process vs. Photosynthesis
The structure and function of Futurefarmers.

Sztafij Solar Water Purifier Unit.
1. Contaminated H$_2$0
2. Elastic pipe connecting kettle
3. Input Chamber
4. Condensing Chamber
5. Pure H$_2$0

^ >
I. 2.
Peter Grundy/Grundy
Northedge
Client: Shell
International
Date: 2000—present

These images form part
of an illustration
identity for a
department within
Shell International
that deals with
forward-thinking via
scenario creation. The
two image sets are
divided into icons
and characters
specifically for use
on-screen and in print
to clarify complex
written explanations
and descriptions. The
sets are added to as
the project develops
and scenarios expand.
The visual system
demonstrates Grundy
Northedge's approach
to problem-solving and
identity design—a
very visual form of
information design.

^ >
I. 2.
Simon Emery
Client: Cinven Venture
Capitalists/Range
Rover
Date: 200I

The leading venture capitalists Cinven commissioned Simon Emery to produce this series of illustrations which would convey key aspects and values that are intrinsic to their business. The images, which address areas such as growth and development, vision and problem-solving, were produced by Emery using a combination of SLR photography, Photoshop and Freehand. The image on the following page is a commission from Range Rover that illustrates their rigorous global test locations.

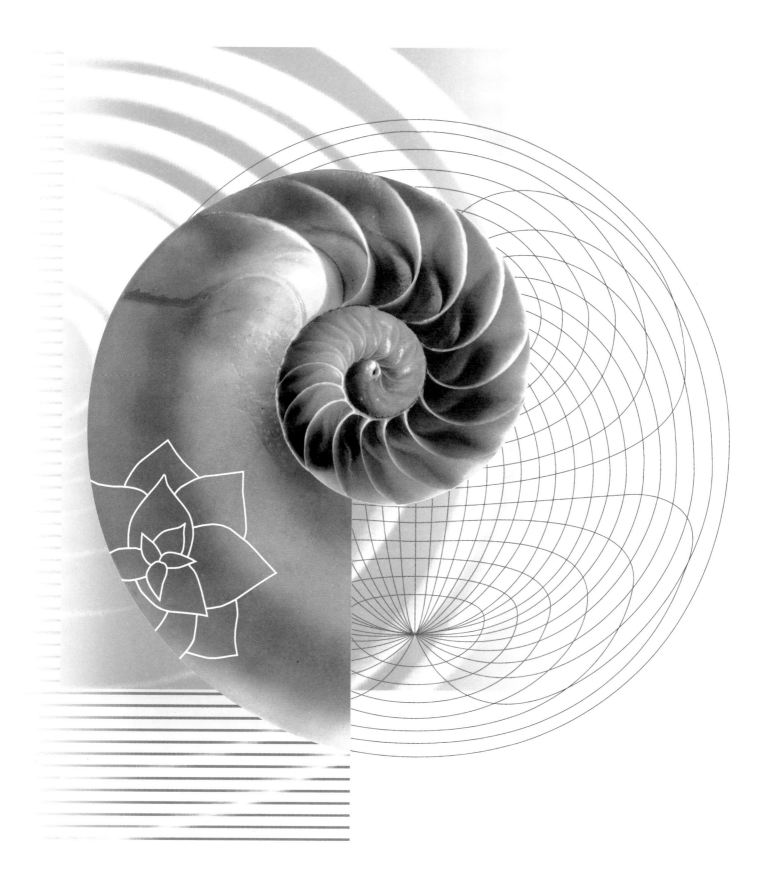

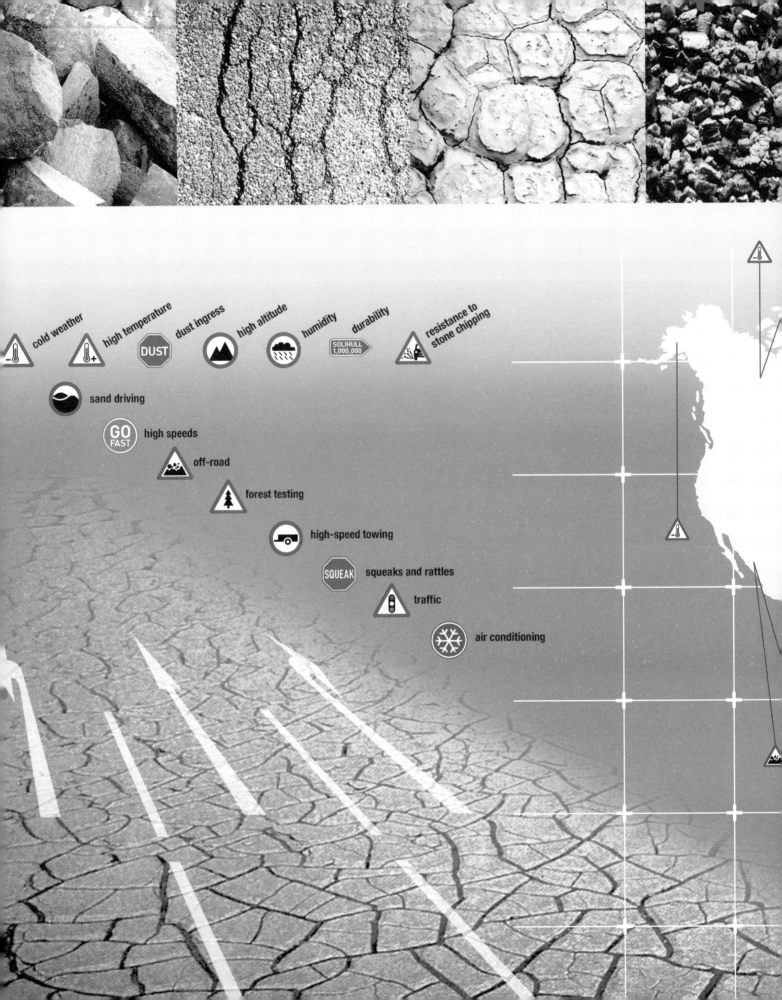

cold weather

high temperature

DUST — dust ingress

high altitude

humidity

SOLIHULL 1,000,000 — durability

resistance to stone chipping

sand driving

GO FAST — high speeds

off-road

forest testing

high-speed towing

SQUEAK — squeaks and rattles

traffic

air conditioning

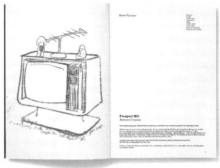

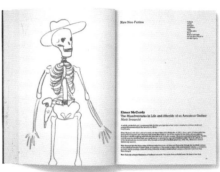

^ ^
I. 2.
Frost Design
Client: Fourth Estate
Date: 2003

The London-based design practice Frost Design have had a long working relationship with the innovative publisher Fourth Estate. Twice a year Frost are asked to produce a new catalog for the next season's titles. Using a different visual theme for each issue, the design group are able to take an unusual approach as the publisher does not require them to feature the front covers of the new books. For this catalog Vince Frost commissioned Marion Deuchars to produce a series of images for each new title. The images she produced appear as if made using carbon copy paper.

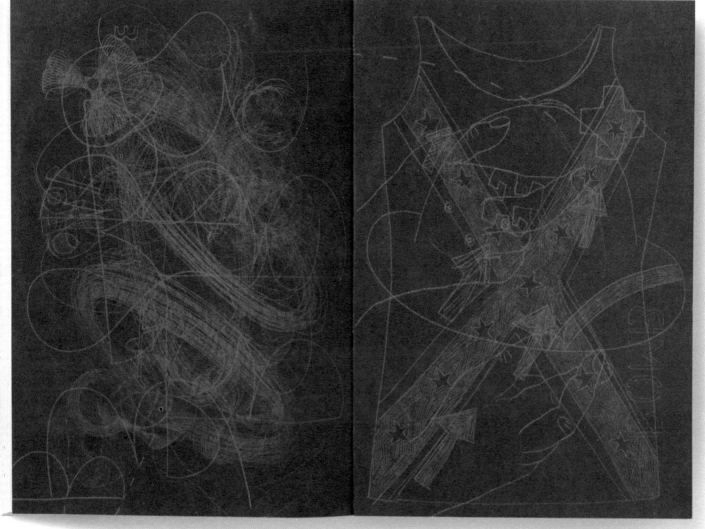

^ ^ > > v
I. 2. 3. 4. 5.
Carter Wong Tomlin
Client: Howies

Illustrators: Andrew
Mockett, Brian Cairns,
Aldous Eveleigh,

Ian Wright,
Richard Beards
Date: 2002

This in-store campaign
for Howies, the t-shirt
company, was created
by UK-based design
group Carter Wong
Tomlin. They took an
unusual approach to
the marketing of the

company, which takes
an active ethical
business stance, and
donates a percentage of
their profits to grass
roots environmental
and social projects.
The theme of recycling

is explored here
through commissioning
the redecoration of
wardrobes. Fourteen
illustrators were asked
to explore a range of
issues central to the
company's philosophy.

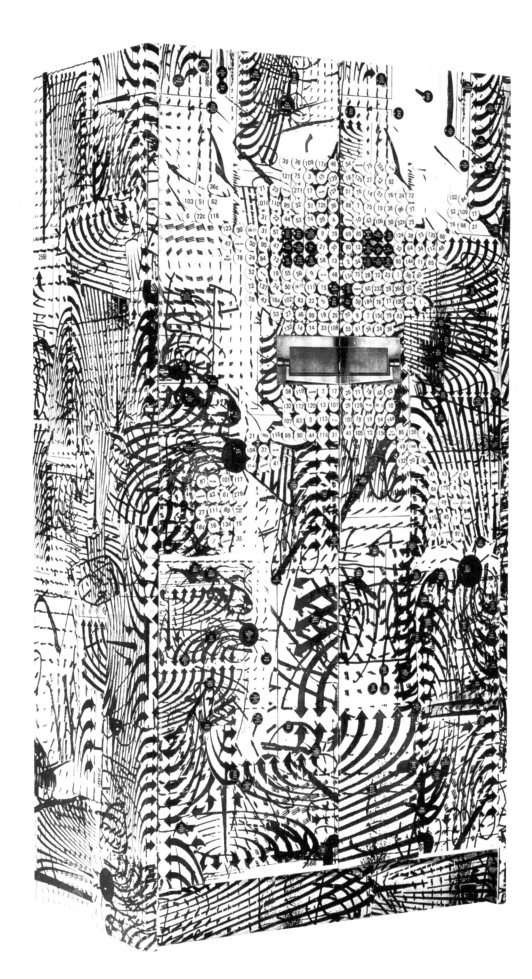

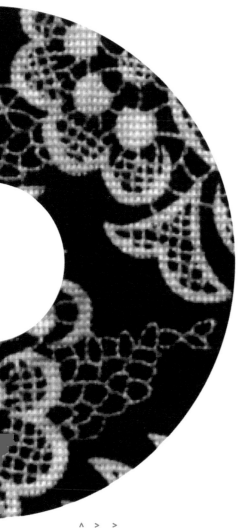

^ > >
I. 2. 3.
Lizzie Finn
Client: The Echo
Label/Chrysalis
Date: I999/2002

These record sleeves, produced by Lizzie Finn for the British band Moloko, were created using soft toy and craft instruction books originally published in the I970s and 80s. Using a combination of mobile-making, sewing, crochet, pom-pom making, and photos manipulated in Photoshop, Finn created this series of images featured on the sleeves, and produced her own typographic forms using similar materials to create the home craft feel.

Picture Perfect: Marion Deuchars

^ ^
I. 2.
Marion Deuchars &
Angus Hyland
Client: The British
Council
Date: 2002

This poster, for Picture This, commissioned by Angus Hyland at Pentagram to promote a British Council touring exhibition in South America, is a playful attempt to represent the notion of Britishness. The exhibition of contemporary illustration was hung in art institutions and colleges, and celebrates clichés of London: pigeons, buses and recognizable monuments. Deuchars produced a series of drawings which were then collaged by Hyland to create the final poster.

CARACAS
EXPOSICIÓN
7 JUNIO - 28 JULIO
MUSEO DE ARTE CONTEMPORÁNEO
DE CARACAS SOFÍA IMBER

BOGOTÁ
EXPOSICIÓN
15 AGOSTO - 7 SEPTIEMBRE
SALA DE INFORMACIÓN,
BIBLIOTECA LUIS ÁNGEL ARANGO
BANCO DE LA REPÚBLICA

SANTIAGO DE CHILE
EXPOSICIÓN
25 SEPTIEMBRE -10 OCTUBRE
GALERÍA DE ARTE CENTRO DE
EXTENSIÓN DE LA PONTIFICIA
UNIVERSIDAD CATÓLICA DE CHILE

PICTURE THIS
EN LATINOAMÉRICA

ILLUSTRACIÓN CONTEMPORÁNEA BRITÁNICA

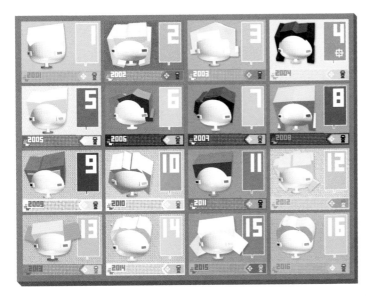

^ ^ > >
I. 2. 3. 4.
Future Farmers
Client: MTV Japan
Date: 2002

Amy Franceschini of the the US-based design group Future Farmers created this identity for MTV Japan. The group were commissioned to produce a set of I6 wallpapers for cellphones, which could be downloaded via the MTV Japan website. Amy Franceschini describes her approach as giving herself "the challenge of designing a new family of 3D characters and a set of cars. It was an excercise for me to step out of my normal 3D aesthetic". The result is a family of I6 Polygonians, so-called because the files were rendered with low quality polygons.

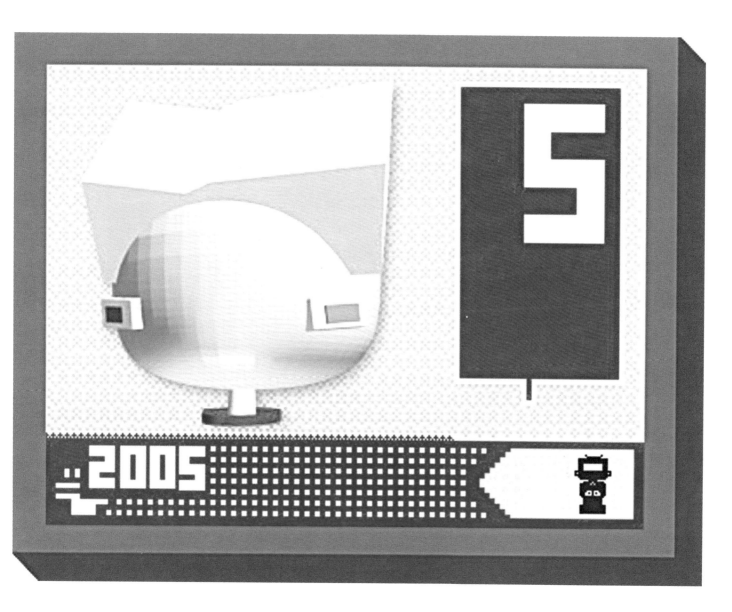

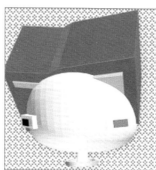
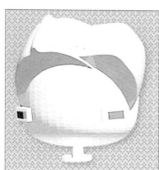

^ ^ >
I. 2. 3.
Paul Bowman
Date: 2000
Client: Paul Bowman

These illustrations are from Paul Bowman's own sketchbooks and visual reference material. Much of his work is influenced by his strong interest in music such as reggae and Northern Soul.

These images were made in direct response to the emotion and excitement of live music. They followed an extended period of working with electronic media and as Bowman says "it gave me the opportunity to draw in a more direct fashion; a way of clearing the pipes" before beginning work again.

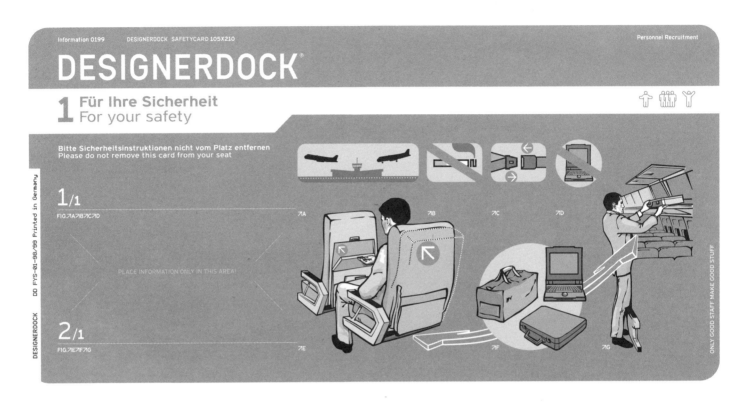

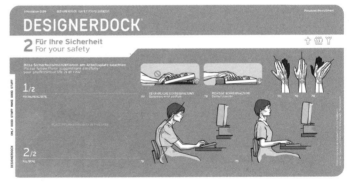

^ ^ >
I. 2. 3.
Stefan Gandl/
Designershock
Client: Designerdock
Date: 1997

This identity, for the specialist creatives' job agency Designerdock, was created by Stefan Gandl in 1997. It plays with analogies to the printed products of airlines and air travel. The flexible, modular structure of the design has been extended and developed annually as the company has expanded and moved to new locations. The DS Ticket font, also created by the group, was originally developed for the Designerdock boarding pass. The peculiar shapes of this font are intended to produce an effect similar to that of needle-printing.

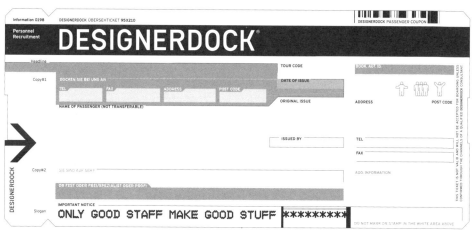

^ >
I. 2.
Rian Hughes
Clients: Deadline 1995,
2000 AD 1994, Xpresso

Rian Hughes has done
more to extend the
definition of an
illustrator than any
other working at
present. The breadth
of projects he has
undertaken range
from animations and
packaging, to music

Books 1990, Judge Dredd
magazine 1993,
DC Comics 1994, 1997,

sleeves and magazine
editorial illustrations.
These logos will be very
familiar to the avid
comic book reader.
Hughes is often
commissioned to develop
much more than a
logotype, often art
directing an entire

1998, Knockabout
Comics 1986, Video
Browser 1990

magazine or comic.

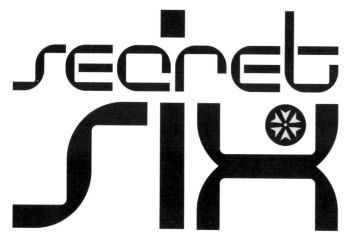

^ ^ > > > >
I. 2. 3. 4. 5. 6.
Yee-Haw Letterpress
Industries
Client: American
Visionary Art Museum
Date: 200I

These Super Soul Tarot Cards were made using scratchboards, which were then converted into etched plates and linocuts, and all hand-printed using letterpress. They celebrate the good guy/bad guy dichotomy of singers such as Al Green and James Brown. Julie Belcher says, "James Brown was an obvious choice to illustrate the Sinner card following his many brushes with the law, but he is still Mr. Dynamite". Otis Redding was selected for the Lost Soul card because "he was killed before his biggest hit, Dock of the Bay, was ever released; he was only 26 years old".

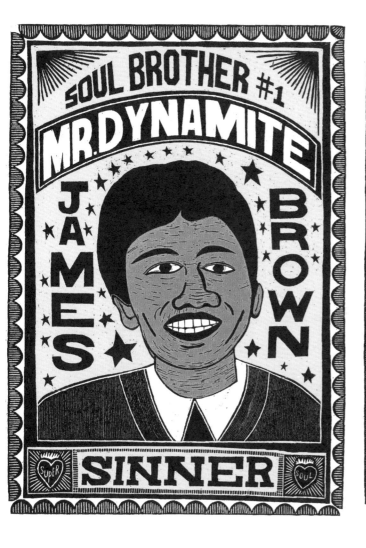

Picture Perfect: Yee-Haw Letterpress Industries

Julie Belcher
Yee-Haw Letterpress Industries, Knoxville, US

Could tell me how the name of the group came about?

Yeeee-Haaaaw! We wanted a good Southern name and it's a great way to answer the phone, it makes folks laugh. Although Kevin's mama didn't think we could get any work with a name like Yee-Haw... but the name Whoop-Ass made her cry so I think we made the right choice.

Your work appears to be a celebration of white trash Country and Western culture. How does this influence your work?

Our approach has always been to start each project with no preconceived boundaries and try to let each piece emerge. What initially brought Kevin into letterpress, and what keeps him doing it, is an obvious first love of typography, especially drawing and carving type into blocks. I wanted a direct hands-on approach to design instead of a sterile computer process. Yee-Haw's technique of combining typography, illustration, and content in a traditional letterpress environment has developed into a stylistic niche that is highly recognizable. Incorporating moveable type as well as carved imagery, typographic and illustrative, is an important part of our process to differentiate our work from screen-printing.

Attitude is very important in a body of work. The key is finding a voice and expressing it on the page, always in a reverent way towards the subject. Kevin creates a sometimes mythical history within the text by combining some true facts with legend which can be factual or pure baloney. He sometimes uses the 'snake oil' approach, extolling virtues for the sake of overkill or boiling the whole thing down to a true southern hillbilly vernacular. Nothing is wasted; we like to call it the 'whole hog' method.

There is a saying that all culture is local; there is a lot of power in working your own soil. In the land of the Appalachians, some of the oldest mountains in the world, the land of Davy Crockett and Daniel Boone, there is a fierce spirit of pride that runs through the people and the places. Early on we even attempted to pander to the geography of America, making New Yorker stuff for New Yorkers, but found that they weren't interested in it, they liked the southern icons which was something we knew more about anyways.

We set out to make the best letterpress products available. Period. We are prolific, we have bills to pay and have found a way to make this a business instead of a hobby. Most of our clients are regular folks and a hand-made product is appreciated but hard on the pocketbook. We try to give our all whether the customer is a small band trying to get an audience, a couple planning their wedding event, or an independent film-maker trying to get their hard work out to the public.

How important is the print/letterpress technology in your work?

The importance of the hand-made print via letterpress cannot be overstated. All of our work is hand-set, hand-carved, and hand-printed. There is the love of the human touch in all of these pieces; of course this is antiquated technology and it's hard to compete in this digital age. Some of our clients have no idea what goes into producing work the old-fashioned way. We think it's very important to keep letterpress alive. Even though we use antique tools for production, we make a contemporary product that speaks to the present.

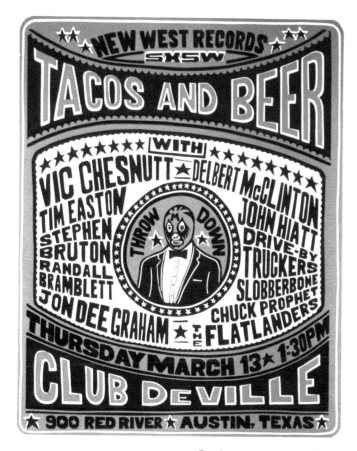

>Poster and print for
a New West Records
concert at SXSW (South
by SouthWest), a music
industry event in
Austin, Texas

>Cover illustration
for Print Magazine.
All text was hand-set
lead type, some carved
artwork, testimonials,
and found photographs.

How do you consider what you do? Is is design? Art?
Illustration? Or perhaps it's not important?

Yee-Haw is a combination of design, art, and
illustration, with some printmaking thrown in the
pot. The walls that separate designers, artists,
and illustrators are non-existent in our studio.
We try to shake off any single label and we like to
mix it all up. We have a company slogan 'Art for
the People' and we live and work by it.

I000 Journals	someguy@I000journals.com	Neasden Control Centre	info@neasdencontrolcentre.com
	www.I000journals.com		www.neasdencontrolcentre.com
Arkitip	connect@arkitip.com	Mark Pawson	mark@mpawson.demon.co.uk
	www.arkitip.com		www.mpawson.demon.co.uk
Bark	tim@barkdesign.net	Pixelhugger	pete@pixelhugger.xom
	www.barkdesign.net		www.pixelhugger.com
Jonathan Barnbrook	www.barnbrook.net	Quickhoney	p@quickhoney.com
	www.virusfonts.com		www.quickhoney.com
Ian Bilbey	www.ianbilbey.com	Rinzen	www.rinzen.com they@rinzen.com
Paul Bowman	bowmani@dircon.co.uk	Andy Simionato	www.thisisamagazine.com
			info@thisisamagazine.com
Anthony Burrill	anthony@friendchip.com	Ward Schumaker	warddraw@best.com
	www.anthonyburrill.com		www.warddraw.com
Carter Wong Tomlin	info@carterwongtomlin.com	THS/Beast	I@ths.nu
	www.carterwongtomlin.com		www.ths.nu
François Chalet	fevrier@primalinea.com	Garth Walker	garth@oj.co.za
	www.primalinea.com/chalet		www.i-jusi.com
Cosmic Debris	www.emilystrange.com	Paul Wearing	paulwearing@illustrator.demon.co.uk
	www.oopsy-daisy.comwww.bonbon-ago-go.com	Alex Williamson	alex.crooked@blueyonder.co.uk
Designershock	stefan@DSOSI.com	Yee-Haw Letterpress	
	www.designershock.com	Industries	julie@yeehawindustries.com
Marion Deuchars	mariondeuchars@lineone.net		www.yeehawindustries.com
	www.mariondeuchars.com		
eBoy	t@eboy.com	Lawrence Zeegen	z@zeegen.com
	www.eboy.com		www.zeegen.com
Simon Emery	semery@mailbox.co.uk		
Shepard Fairey	info@obeygiant.com		
	www.obeygiant.com		
Lizzie Finn	lizzie@lizziefinn.com		
	www.lizziefinn.com		
Frost Design	info@frostdesign.co.uk		
	www.frostdesign.co.uk		
Future Farmers	ame@mindspring.com		
	www.futurefarmers.com		
Gobler Toys	iragobler@aol.com		
	www.goblertoys.com		
Jasper Goodall	jasper.goodall@bigactive.com		
	www.bigactive.com		
Peter Grundy	peter@grundynorthedge.com		
	www.grundynorthedge.com		
Rian Hughes	rianhughes@aol.com		
	www.devicefonts.co.uk		
Nathan Jurevicius	nejurk@bigpond.com		
	www.nathanj.com.aus		
	www.scarygirl.com		
Kabeljau	info@kabeljau.ch		
	www.kabeljau.ch		

Big Mouth Strikes Again!
Thanks are necessary to the people involved in making this project happen: To the many illustrators and designers who contributed work and gave up their time to take part. To my long-time collaborator Russell Bestley for working so patiently with me on the design and layout of the book. To Becky Moss and Kate Shanahan for the editorial advice and genuinely hard work— above and beyond the call of duty. To Paul Bowman for our many conversations about illustration during the development of the book.

To Susan, Audra, and Eugene: THANK YOU.